英汉口译教程系列

实用英汉酒店口译

张积模　江美娜 ◎编著

化学工业出版社

·北京·

内容简介

本书由数十年来执教于英语口译教学一线并活跃于大型国际活动现场的两位作者精心编著而成。他们本着实用第一的原则，根据酒店口译最常见的场景将内容划分为 10 个单元，每个单元包括课文 1 和课文 2 两部分，每部分进一步细分为"对话中英互译""短文英译中""短文中译英"三节。在 10 个单元有针对性的口译训练之后，最后的附录部分又列出了作者多年亲身实践积累得来的 16 条宝贵口译对策。

本书内容设置合理，科学实用，配标准美式录音，既可以作为大学生、研究生口译教材或口译教材的补充材料，也可以作为职业培训教材，还可以作为特定专业学生提高英语听力水平、口语能力的课外读物，可谓一书多用。

图书在版编目(CIP)数据

实用英汉酒店口译/张积模，江美娜编著. —北京：化学工业出版社，2021.12
英汉口译教程系列
ISBN 978-7-122-40035-2

Ⅰ.①实… Ⅱ.①张… ②江… Ⅲ.①饭店-英语-口译-高等职业教育-教材 Ⅳ.①F719.2

中国版本图书馆 CIP 数据核字（2021）第 201540 号

责任编辑：王丽丽　丁　瑞　　　　　　　　装帧设计：史利平
责任校对：杜杏然

出版发行：化学工业出版社（北京市东城区青年湖南街 13 号　邮政编码 100011）
印　　装：三河市延风印装有限公司
710mm×1000mm　1/16　印张 11½　字数 233 千字　2022 年 5 月北京第 1 版第 1 次印刷

购书咨询：010-64518888　　　　　　　　　　售后服务：010-64518899
网　　址：http://www.cip.com.cn
凡购买本书，如有缺损质量问题，本社销售中心负责调换。

定　　价：39.80 元　　　　　　　　　　　　　　　　　版权所有　违者必究

前　言

说到外语学习，人们自然会想到翻译。说到翻译，自然会想到口译。说到口译，自然会想到交替传译或同声传译。

随着经济全球化的加速，社会对口译人才的需求越来越大，要求也越来越高。很多外语专业的学生把成为合格的同传译员作为自己追求的最高目标，非英语专业的学生也紧随其后，纷纷加入到口译员的行列中来。然而，现实情况又如何呢？

我国学英语的人数高达几亿，但真正能用英语工作的人并不多，能够作口译的更是少之又少。很多人在从事口译工作，然而称职的没有多少，优秀的就更是寥寥无几。这究竟是什么原因呢？

主要是因为社会上对英语学习本身的误解。大部分人都把英语当成知识来学，把活生生的语言变成了枯燥的语法规则的掌握和单词量的积累，忽视了或者根本没有意识到学英语是一种能力的培养。有很多译员拥有大学英语四、六级证书或专业英语四、八级证书，有的还参加了各种口译证书的培训，可是，就是这样一群精英人士常常连基本的英文自我介绍都做不好，连个简单的名片都写不对。奇怪吗？一点都不奇怪。这是因为四六级也好，专四专八也罢，反映出来的统统是"应试能力"，而口译是"应用能力"的真实体现。一字之差，天壤之别！

现在，大部分高校的英语系都开设了口译课，有硕士点的学校还开设了同声传译。口译教程也是琳琅满目，但良莠不齐，欧式汉语、中式英语充斥着课本，让学习者无所适从。

众所周知，口译不是教出来的，是练出来的。口译能力的培养靠的是时间投入与大量练习，别无他法。笔者根据多年口译教学和口译实践经验，编写了这本口译实用教材。该教材以酒店为主题，这样，既方便了相应领域的口译人员，又方便了口译自学者，可以针对性地反复练习，达到熟能生巧的目的。该书既可以作为大学生口译教材或口译教材的补充材料，又可以作为职业培训教材，还可以作为特定专业学生提高英语听力水平、口语能力的课外读物，可谓一书多用。

本书在编写过程中参考了国内外大量网站的资料，在此一并致谢。由于时间仓促，加上笔者能力有限，疏漏在所难免，欢迎本书使用者不吝金玉，批评指正。

张积模

2021 年 5 月

目录 | Contents

第 1 单元　预订房间　Room Reservations　/ 1

第 2 单元　行李服务　Luggage Service　/ 16

第 3 单元　办理入住　Reception and Check-in　/ 29

第 4 单元　送餐服务　Room Service　/ 44

第 5 单元　客房服务　Housekeeping Service　/ 58

第 6 单元　餐厅就餐　At a Restaurant　/ 74

第 7 单元　兑换外币　Foreign Currency Exchange　/ 87

第 8 单元　购物中心　At the Store　/ 101

第 9 单元　美容美发　At the Beauty Salon　/ 117

第 10 单元　投诉处理　Handling Complaints　/ 133

附录　口译对策　Coping Tactics　/ 148

第1单元
预订房间

Room Reservations

课文 1　　Text A

Section Ⅰ: Dialog

Interpret the following dialog alternatively into English and Chinese.

服务员：InterContinental Qingdao. Can I help you, sir?

客人：我是从香港打来的。嗯，我从朋友那里得到你们的号码，他一个月前在你们那里住过。他说，你们位于奥帆中心，对吗？

服务员：You are right, sir.

客人：那我找对了。嗯……嗯……

服务员：Well, excuse me, sir, are you looking for a room or...

客人：找房间。对了，你们是几星级的？

服务员：We're actually the only five-star hotel at the Center. What kind of room would you like, sir?

客人：我想订一个双人间。

服务员：A double Room. For which dates, sir?

客人：25 号到 30 号。

服务员：Let me check for you, sir. ... Sorry, sir, we don't have any double rooms available for those dates.

客人：噢，太可惜了。

服务员：How many in your party, sir?

客人：两位，我和我夫人。

服务员：I see. If you still want to stay in our hotel, how about you stay in a triple room? We still have two available.

客人：让我想想。嗯，差价是多少？

服务员：You need to pay an extra 180 yuan.

客人：180。嗯，我想要一个带海景的房间，不知道……

服务员：Don't worry, sir. Both are rooms with a nice view of the sea, only that one has a front view and the other, a rear view.

客人：我喜欢朝阳面的。

服务员：No problem. May I have your name, sir?

客人：巴拉克·奥巴马。

服务员：What? The President of the United States? You must be kidding, sir.

客人：我没开玩笑，小姐。我不是美国总统奥巴马，我是音乐家奥巴马。

旅客提供各种需求，包括食宿，为旅客的坐骑提供马厩和饲料，为邮车更换马匹等。典型的客栈包括一个内院，两边有卧房，前面有厨房和客厅，后面有马厩。

17 世纪中期以来的约 200 年间，驿站马车旅馆成为驿站旅客歇脚的地方。驿站马车旅馆为驿站马车和邮车的马匹提供马厩，更换马匹。从传统上看，驿站马车旅馆之间相隔七英里，但这在很大程度上取决于不同的地形。

在英国的一些城镇，一个镇上就有十个这样的旅馆，它们之间的竞争非常激烈。为了收入，一方面要争夺驿站马车运营商，另一方面也要争夺富有的旅客，为他们提供饮食。到该世纪末，驿站马车旅馆运营得更为专业，有常规的时间表，也有固定的菜单。

18 世纪中叶，旅馆开始迎合富裕客户的需求，因而店面越来越宏伟壮观，服务水平越来越上档次。

19 世纪，酒店在西欧和北美遍地开花，豪华酒店在该世纪后期开始出现，迎合富商巨贾的需求。

今天，你可以找到各种各样的酒店，迎合不同人的口味、不同的消费水准。

Section Ⅲ: Passage

Hotel Rating (Part One)

Star ratings are systems that rank hotels according to quality. Star rating systems are intended to serve as a guideline for guests when making reservations. While star ratings can be helpful when booking rooms, there is no standardized star rating system so far. In Europe, they are ranked from one to five stars, with five stars being the highest rating possible. The same applies in the United States, but an incremental half star may be given where for example two stars is better than standard but does not warrant three stars, etc.

In order to promote the development of tourism and protect the interests of tourists, some relatively unified standards have been formulated to designate hotels. Thus, they are compared and classified according to facilities, scale, service quality and management. In China, they are generally classified into star-rated hotels, boutique accommodations, service apartments, comfort inns, Chinese courtyards and hostels.

Star Rating

Star-rated hotels are those which have been approved by the National Tourism Administration in the star-rating hotel assessment. Normally, they provide better facilities and service than non-rated ones. In China, accommodations can be rated as one, two, three, four or five stars.

Quasi-star Rating

The term "quasi-star rating" is not a true rating. In some cities, the use of quasi-star rating is forbidden by the Industrial and Commercial Bureau and Tourism Administration.

The quasi-star system is ambiguous and may refer to an accommodation built according to a certain star standard but has not been assessed by the National Tourism Administration. Therefore there is no guarantee that it meets the criteria for such a rating. However, the travel industry widely uses quasi-star ratings. It is a fact that there are differences between a quasi-star rated and a true star-rated hotel. Generally, a quasi-5 star one can be considered as 4 stars or a little better. A quasi-4 star one can be considered as 3 stars or a little better, and so forth. Until an accommodation has been operating for one year, it has no right to apply for the star-rating hotel assessment. Consequently, even if it has been built according to the five star standards we can only consider it as a quasi-5 star one at most.

5-Star Hotels

They offer only the highest level of accommodation and services. The properties offer a high degree of personal service. Although most five star hotels are large properties, sometimes the small independent (non-chain) property offers an elegant intimacy that can not be achieved in the larger setting. Their locations can vary from the very exclusive locations of a suburban area to the heart of downtown. The lobbies are sumptuous, the rooms complete with stylish furnishing and quality linens. The amenities often include VCRs, CD stereos, garden tubs, heated pools and an in-room video library and more. They feature up to three restaurants all with exquisite menus. Room service is usually available 24 hours a day. Fitness Centers and valet and/or garage parking are typically available. A concierge is also available to assist you.

4-Star Hotels

They are mostly large, formal accommodations with smart reception areas, front desk service and bellhop service. Usually, they are located near accommodations of the same caliber and neighbor shopping malls, dining areas and other major attractions. The level of service is well above average and the rooms are well lit and furnished. Restaurant dining is usually available and may include more than one choice. Some properties will offer continental breakfast and/or happy hour delicacies. Room service is usually available on a 24 hour basis. Valet parking and/or garage service is also usually available. Concierge services, fitness centers and one or more pools are often provided.

 **Text B**

Section I: Dialog

Interpret the following dialog alternatively into English and Chinese.

服务员：Reservations. May I help you, sir?

客人：我想在你们酒店订一个单人间。

服务员：Is that Mr. Smith?

客人：是的，我是约翰·史密斯。小姐，您是……?

服务员：Wang. May Wang.

客人：哦，梅，是你啊。太巧了!

服务员：I recognized your voice the moment you spoke.

客人：谢谢，梅。你这么一说，我很高兴。

服务员：How long will you be staying with us this time?

客人：3、4 天吧。我来这儿休个短假。我要一个单人间。

服务员：Just a minute, please. Let's see if there are any rooms available. You know, this is a peak tourist season now.

客人：当然。

服务员：Since you are our regular customer, we are only too pleased to accommodate you. But, unfortunately, all the single rooms are booked up, John.

客人：太糟糕了。双人间还有吗?

服务员：Double rooms? Let me check. Sorry, John, they are all booked up also.

客人：这个时候让我去哪儿找房间? 你知道，我每次来，只住你们酒店。梅，你有什么好办法吗?

服务员：Well, there's a four-star hotel just across the street. A newly-built one that boasts the usual collection of 5-star facilities. So you can enjoy the comfort and convenience of a five-star hotel with the money you will spend in a four-star one.

客人：这倒是个好主意。你有那个酒店的电话号码吗?

服务员：Yes. So you want me to book a room there for you, right?

客人：是的。

服务员：OK. Hold on a second.

(2 分钟后)

服务员：OK, done. Sorry to have kept you waiting, John.
客人：多谢了，梅。我欠你一个大人情。
服务员：Don't mention it. What are friends for?

Section Ⅱ: Passage
Interpret the following passage into Chinese.

Different Qualities That a Hotel Manager Needs

Managing a hotel, regardless of its size or rating, requires a myriad of skills combined with the ability to quickly adapt to changing situations. Hotel managers rarely have two days at work that are remotely similar and have to constantly change their lists of priorities to ensure smooth day-to-day operations.

Communication Skills

To efficiently run a hotel and keep guests happy enough to return, a hotel manager needs exemplary communication skills with his staff as well as his guests. He must clearly delegate tasks through oral communications and provide constructive guidance to new employees. A good rapport with guests of various ages from many ethnic and socioeconomic backgrounds builds good will and increases repeat business. Expertise in written communications is required to answer inquiries, develop corporate contacts and negotiate with vendors and suppliers.

Problem-Solving Capabilities

Whenever a problem arises, the hotel manager is typically the person depended upon to solve it. Whether it's a problem with the inventory of sheets and towels, a complaint about housekeeping service or a discrepancy in room or service charges, the manager has to address it with expedience, professionalism and resolve. He must be fair in his assessments and strive to satisfy guests without adversely affecting the hotel's profits or reputation.

Attention to Detail

From the moment a hotel manager steps across the threshold when his shift begins, he has to observe all surroundings to ensure the hotel is in pristine condition. From the cleanliness of the front door to the attire of the staff, his attention to detail helps identify and maintain the highest standards. Hotel managers typically spot-check rooms to guarantee their cleanliness and recognize old or worn furniture and accessories that require replacement. As he interacts with guests and watches his staff deal with the public, he must closely observe body language and expressions to determine if the patrons seem satisfied with their accommodations.

Financial Acumen

As with any business, the bottom line lies in the profits. Hotel managers review daily, weekly and monthly records of reservations, invoices, cancellations, complaints and income from fringe sources such as hotel gift shops and in-house restaurants and bars. He needs good analytical skills to identify areas of financial loss as well as develop and recommend viable plans to make them profitable. A hotel manager has to prepare clear and concise profit and margin statements for review by investors and upper management, so skills in math, statistics and the creation of computerized spreadsheets are necessary.

Section Ⅲ: Passage
Interpret the following passage into English.

酒店评级制度（第二部分）

三星级酒店

三星级酒店通常提供更加宽敞的空间，包括装修精美的客房和大堂。一般不提供行李服务。它们往往位于主要高速公路或者商业区附近，购物方便，去中高档价位的景点也方便。一般而言，它们有中型餐厅，提供早餐、午餐和晚餐。送餐服务因酒店而异。提供代客泊车服务。此外，还有健身中心和游泳池。

二星级酒店

它们通常是独立的、名牌连锁旅馆，有着良好的设施。旅馆面积不大，或者中等，前往中等价位的景点比较方便。旅馆设施通常包括电话和电视。其中一些提供有限的就餐服务。不过，不提供送餐服务和行李服务。

一星级酒店

一星级酒店通常是规模不大的小旅馆，由业主管理。一般是2至4层楼高，私人气氛浓厚。它们往往离经济景点很近，离主要路口和公交车站也不远。只提供基本的旅馆设施，室内陈设整洁干净。大部分旅馆不提供就餐服务，不过，离一些物美价廉的餐馆不远，走着去就可以了。电视节目过了某个钟点可能会受到限制。

精品酒店

与传统的星级酒店不同，精品酒店强调个性。成功的精品酒店一般有三个特点，即独立精神、个性品质和文化遗产。通常，这种酒店拥有丰富的地方文化风味和独特的历史记忆。住在这样的酒店里，客人能得到无与伦比的享受，这可是星级酒店无法企及的。

酒店式公寓

酒店式公寓起源于1994年的欧洲，提供酒店式服务和公寓式管理。它曾经是租给景区游客暂时休息的地方。既具备住宿的性质，又具备"临时住所"的功能，酒店式公寓开始成形。

酒店式公寓提供独立的卧室、一个客厅、一个或多个洗手间以及一个设施齐全的厨房，以便客人自己做饭。住在这样的地方，客人不仅可以享受到细心的服务，而且可以享受到家的自由。

舒适酒店

走进一家舒适酒店，你马上会感到轻松自在。你会注意到温暖的氛围和个性化的周到服务。晚上，你可以舒舒服服地睡上一觉，第二天起来，神清气爽。舒适酒店不同于招待所和接待中心，它们是一种新型的连锁机构，提供国际标准服务。他们关注的是那些希望物有所值的经济型游客。在这里，你总能以适中的价格获得满意的服务。

四合院酒店

四合院是古代中国人特有的一种建筑，一个院子四面建有房屋，通常由正房、东西厢房等组成。近来，越来越多的庭院改造成了酒店，接待来自世界各地的客人。四合院一般具有古典东方建筑的韵味。住在那里，客人不仅可以领略传统的氛围，也可以更好地了解中国的历史。

Section I: Dialog

服务员：客房预订。需要帮忙吗，先生？

客人：Yes. I'd like to book a single room in your hotel.

服务员：您是史密斯先生吧？

客人：Yes, this is John Smith. Miss...?

服务员：我姓王。我叫王梅。

客人：Oh, May, it's you. What a coincidence!

服务员：您一开口，我就听出您的声音来了。

客人：Thank you, May. It's very sweet of you to say so.

服务员：您这次打算住多久？

客人：Three or four days. I'm here for a short break. A single room, please.

服务员：请稍等，我看看还有没有房间。您知道，现在是旅游旺季。

客人：Naturally.

服务员：您是我们的老客户，我们很愿意为您服务。不过，不幸的是，约翰，所有的单人间都预订一空。

客人：That's too bad. Any double rooms left?

服务员：双人间？ 我查查。不好意思，约翰，全预订出去了。

客人：Where am I going to find a room at this time of day? You see, yours is the only hotel I stay in each time I am here. So, what do you recommend, May?

服务员：嗯，街对面有一家四星级酒店，新开的，设施都是五星级的。所以，您可以花四星级的钱享受五星级的舒适与便利。

客人：Sounds a neat idea. Do you happen to have the number of the hotel?

服务员：有的。您是想让我帮您在那儿订一个房间吗？

客人：Yes, please.

服务员：好的，请稍等。

（2分钟后）

服务员：好了，行了。不好意思，约翰，让您久等了。

客人：Thanks a lot, May. I owe you a big one.

服务员：区区小事，不足挂齿。朋友是用来干吗的？

Section Ⅱ：Passage

酒店经理需要具备的素质

管理一个酒店，无论大小等级，都需要大量的技能，以快速适应不断变化的情况。酒店经理每天的工作都是不一样的，必须不断修订"优先任务清单"，确保日常工作的平稳进行。

沟通能力

为了有效地管理酒店，让客人自愿成为回头客，酒店经理需要拥有与客人和员工有效沟通的能力。他必须通过口头交流，清清楚楚地把任务分配下去，给新员工提供建设性指导。与来自不同种族、不同社会经济背景的不同年龄段的客人建立良好关系，可以树立良好的信誉，增加回头客。酒店经理还需要书面沟通方面的专业知识，回答客人的问题，与企业建立关系，与卖主、供应商进行谈判。

解决问题的能力

每当出现问题时，人们通常依赖酒店经理来解决。无论是床单、毛巾的库存问题，客房服务投诉问题，还是房费或服务费出现了问题，经理必须凭借专业知识、以适当的方式毫不犹豫地去解决。他在评估时必须持公平态度，在努力满足客人的前提下，不损害酒店的利益和声誉。

对细节的关注

酒店经理从跨过门槛开始接班之时起，必须观察环境，确保酒店处于原先的状态。从正门的洁净度，到员工的服装，其对细节的关注有助于确保和维护酒店最高水准。酒店经理通常要抽查房间，确保其整洁干净，发现陈旧的或磨损的家具及饰品，及时更换。与客人接触时，或观察员工与客人打交道时，酒店经理必须注意客人的肢体语言和面部表情，确定客人对住宿是否满意。

理财智慧

正如任何一种生意一样，酒店业务的底线在于赢得利润。酒店经理每天、每周、每月都要审核预约记录、发票记录、预约取消记录、客人投诉记录以及源自店内礼品店、餐馆和酒吧的额外收入记录。他需要有良好的分析能力，发现亏损的领域，开发并提出可行的计划，让酒店扭亏为盈。酒店经理必须为投资者和上层管理人员准备清晰、简洁的利润报表，所以，数学、统计学以及计算机电子表格创建能力是必不可少的。

Section Ⅲ：Passage

Hotel Rating（Part Two）

3-Star Hotels

Typically they offer more spacious accommodations that include well appointed rooms and decorated lobbies. It is not usual for them to provide bellhop service. They are often located near major expressways or business areas, convenient to shopping and moderate to high priced attractions. Usually, they feature medium-sized restaurants that typically offer service from breakfast through dinner. Room service availability may vary. Valet parking, fitness centers and pools are often provided.

2-Star Hotels

They are usually independent and name brand hostel chains with a reputation for offering consistent quality amenities. It is usually small to medium-sized and conveniently located to moderately priced attractions. The facilities typically include telephones and TV's in the bedroom. Some of them offer limited restaurant service; however, room service and bellhop service are not provided as a rule.

1-Star Hotels

They are typically smaller hostels managed by the proprietor. It is often 2-4 stories high and usually has a more personal atmosphere. It's usually located near affordable attractions, major intersections and convenient to public transportation. Furnishings and facilities are clean but basic. Most will not have a restaurant on site but are usually within walking distance to some good low-priced dining. Public access, past certain hours, may be restricted.

Boutique Hotels

Different from traditional star-rated ones, boutique hotels emphasize individuality. Successful ones always have three characteristics, namely, independent spirit, personality traits and cultural heritage. And generally this kind of accommodation boasts both the rich flavor of local culture and a unique historical memory of it. When staying in such accommodations, guests can have unparalleled enjoyment which is lacking in star-rated hotels.

Service Apartments

The service apartment, which originated in 1994 in Europe, provides hotel-style services and apartment-style management. It used to be leased to tourists for temporary resting in a tourist area. With the nature of an accommodation and the function of "temporary dwelling", the service apartment took shape.

A service apartment provides separate bedrooms, a living room, a bathroom or bathrooms and an equipped kitchen to facilitate self-catering. Staying in such accommodation enables the guests to enjoy not only its attentive service, but also the freedoms of home.

Comfort Inns

The moment you walk into a Comfort Inn, you'll feel at ease. You'll notice the warm atmosphere and the personal, helpful service. You'll appreciate the good night's rest and start the next day refreshed. Comfort Inns differ from hostels and reception centers as they are a new kind of chain-operated establishment providing an internationally standard service. They pay attention to budget travelers who now expect value for money. Here, you will always receive satisfactory service at a moderate price.

Chinese Courtyards

The Chinese Courtyard is a typical quadrangle dwelling as used by ancient Chinese. A courtyard always consists of a central main building and two wing buildings on either side. Recently, more and more courtyards have been converted into hotels to accommodate guests from all over the world. A Courtyard generally has the beauty of classical oriental buildings, where guests can not only enjoy the traditional atmosphere but also learn more about the history of China.

第2单元
行李服务

Luggage Service

 **Text A**

Section Ⅰ: Dialog
Interpret the following dialog alternatively into English and Chinese.

行李员: Good afternoon, ma'am. Welcome to Haitian Hotel.
客人: 谢谢。
行李员: How many pieces of luggage do you have, ma'am?
客人: 3件。
行李员: Two suitcases and a traveling bag?
客人: 是的,没错。
行李员: Just a moment, ma'am. I'll get a luggage cart.
客人: 好的。
行李员: All right. I'll show you to the Front Desk. This way, please.
(10分钟后)
行李员: Finished, ma'am? OK. Let me show you to your room. What's your room number?
客人: 321.
行李员: OK. We'll go up by elevator.
客人: 谢谢。如果您不介意的话,先生,我能给您提个醒吗?
行李员: Yes, ma'am.
客人: 你看,这个旅行箱里有易碎的东西,请小心。
行李员: I will, ma'am. Would you follow me? Your elevator is this way.
客人: 好的,谢谢。
行李员: All right. Here we are at your room, ma'am.
客人: 噢,电梯很稳,一点感觉没有。
行李员: Yes. We replaced the old one last month.
客人: 怪不得,崭新的。
行李员: Where shall I put your luggage, ma'am?
客人: 就放地板上吧。我马上打开。
行李员: OK. There you go.
客人: 谢谢,先生。
行李员: My pleasure, ma'am. If there's nothing else, I think I'll leave you alone.
客人: 谢谢,您想得真周到。

行李员：You are welcome, ma'am. Have a good rest. Goodbye.
客人：再见。

Section Ⅱ: Passage
Interpret the following passage into Chinese.

Duties of a Hotel Concierge

Usually employed by more upscale hotels in major cities like New York, Paris, Los Angeles and Toronto, hotel concierges must be cordial and professional with all hotel guests before and during their stays. She is completely responsible for their satisfaction while they are guests. A concierge facilitates special reservations, provides information about the property's events and amenities, acts as a travel liaison and answers her guests' myriad questions.

Books Special Accommodations

Although most upscale hotels use reservation agents to book most of their rooms, a hotel concierge will help reserve special suites for frequent and returning guests. These guests are often treated with a higher degree of customer service than average guests, so a savvy hotel concierge knows to reserve suites that contain luxury amenities they require, such as Jacuzzi bathtubs and 50-inch plasma TVs.

Provides Hotel, City Information

One of the primary duties of a hotel concierge is to inform hotel guests about events specific to the hotel. For instance, if a wine-tasting event is taking place, the concierge lets the guest know and directs her to the correct location. She may also inform certain guests of private events not open to regular guests. The concierge is the go-to person for information about the city's points of interest, best restaurants, shopping and nightclubs.

Facilitates Travel

Many businesspeople regularly frequent hotels, so a concierge must offer up-to-date travel information. This can entail informing the business traveler about the best flight to a specific city in order for him to arrive ahead of schedule. The concierge also calls airports and train and ship lines to ensure proper reservations.

Solves Problems

When a guest loses his wallet or needs special dry-cleaning services, the concierge handles these needs and emergencies. He also assists when a guest cannot get the special hotel room she requested. Another duty can be to arrange to find baby sitters if parents need to leave their children at the hotel for any reason.

Section Ⅲ: Passage

Interpret the following passage into English.

如何做一名合格的行李员

行李员，又叫侍者，是酒店员工的一个类型。酒店客人一旦办完入住手续，行李员通常会拿上客人的行李，送客人去房间，回答途中客人可能提出的任何问题。行李员也帮助退房客人把行李搬到他们的车、出租车或其他运输工具上。归根结底，行李员的工作集顾客服务与体力劳动于一身。然而，一个优雅的酒店氛围要求行李员展示优秀的工作礼仪。

1. 保持身体健康。要吃好，保证充足的锻炼。不仅穿起制服要好看，更重要的是，替客人拿行李时，要显得十分轻松，还不会拉伤自己。当然，如果可能的话，应尽量使用行李车。

2. 看上去无可挑剔。努力超越预期，把自己最好的状态展现出来。确保制服总是熨烫整齐，鞋子光亮如新，头发干净整洁。

3. 对酒店及房间了如指掌，熟悉店内所有设施及其特点。这样，当客人提出疑问时，你就可以做到心中有数对答如流了，因为客人的问题总是免不了的。

4. 主动帮助客人。如果客人问你如何使用房间里的 DVD 播放器或者如何购买市内一场大型演出的票，你可以告诉他具体步骤。如果你不知道如何帮助客人，要有礼貌，请求懂行的人去帮助他。

5. 微笑待人，和蔼可亲，态度积极专业。你的工作就是要协助客人在住宿期间生活愉快；这当然包括帮助他们搬运行李，但也包括对客人要有温暖、专业和尊敬的态度，这会让他们愿意一次又一次光顾你们的酒店。

6. 提前想到客人的需求。不要等到客人和沉重的行李较劲时，才去找行李员。任何一个客户或潜在客户带着行李抵达酒店或离开酒店时，都要主动提供帮助。

7. 永远听从领班或领导的指示，随叫随到。要让领班知道你在哪里，如何和你取得联系。领班会根据需要给你分配任务。

参考答案

Section Ⅰ: Dialog

行李员：夫人，下午好。欢迎下榻海天大酒店。

客人：Thank you.

行李员：夫人，您一共有几件行李？

客人：Three.

行李员：2个旅行箱，1个旅行包？

客人：Yes. You are right.

行李员：请稍等，夫人，我去取行李车。

客人：OK.

行李员：好了，请跟我到前台。这边请。

(10分钟后)

行李员：办好了吗，夫人？ 好的，让我送您去房间吧。您的房间号码是什么？

客人：321.

行李员：好的。我们坐电梯上去。

客人：Thank you. If you don't mind, can I just give you a warning, sir?

行李员：可以，夫人。

客人：You see, there's something fragile in this suitcase. Please handle it with care.

行李员：我会的，夫人。请跟我来。您的电梯在这边。

客人：OK, thanks.

行李员：好了，到您房间了，夫人。

客人：Oh, the elevator is smooth and steady. I didn't feel a thing.

行李员：是的。上个月刚换的。

客人：No wonder. It's brand new.

行李员：行李放哪儿，夫人？

客人：Just put them on the floor. I'll unpack them right away.

行李员：好的，行了。

客人：Thank you, sir.

行李员：不客气，夫人。要是没有别的事情，我想我该走了。

客人：Thank you. How very thoughtful of you!

行李员：不客气，夫人。好好休息。再见。

客人：Bye.

Section Ⅱ：Passage

酒店礼宾部的职责

通常，像纽约、巴黎、洛杉矶和多伦多这样大城市里的高档酒店会有礼宾部。礼宾人员在客人入住之前和入住期间都必须和蔼可亲、专业、爱岗、一心一意为客人负责，让客人满意。礼宾人员简化特殊预订手续，提供酒店工作安排和便利设施方面的信息，并且，作为旅游联络人，回答客人各种各样的问题。

接受特殊预订

尽管大多数高档酒店是通过预订代理预订大部分房间的，但礼宾部可以协助为频繁往返的客人预订特别套房。这些客人通常比普通客人接受更高级别的待遇。所以，一个精明的礼宾人员知道提前留出这些特殊客人所需的配有豪华设施的套房，包括按摩浴缸、50英寸等离子电视等。

提供酒店、城市信息

酒店礼宾部的一个主要职责，就是通知客人酒店里的一些特殊安排。例如，如果店内有品酒会，礼宾人员会及时通知客人，并把客人带到正确的地点，也会通知部分特定客人一些对普通客人不开放的私人活动。礼宾人员还是客人了解该市旅游景馆、最好餐馆、购物场所和夜总会等的不二人选。

提供旅游便利

许多商人经常下榻酒店，所以，礼宾部必须提供最新的旅行信息。这可能包括为商务旅行者提供前往某市的最佳航班，以便于客人提前到达。礼宾人员也会给机场、火车站和轮船码头打电话，确保为客人订到合适的票。

解决问题

当客人丢失了钱包或需要特殊的干洗服务时，礼宾部会处理这些需求和紧急情况。当客人无法订到其所要求的特殊房间时，礼宾人员也要提供帮助。他们还有一个职责是，若父母因某种原因需要把孩子留在酒店里时，为孩子安排保姆。

Section Ⅲ: Passage

How to Be a Good Bellman

A bellman, also known as a bellhop, is a type of hotel employee. Once hotel guests check in, the bellman usually carries the guests' bags, shows them to their room and answers any questions that the guests might pose on the way to the room. Bellmen also help guests who are checking out to take their bags from the hotel room to their car or who are awaiting a taxi or other mode of transportation. At its core, a bellman's job combines customer service and manual work; however, a typical elegant hotel atmosphere requires bellmen to demonstrate excellent manners on the job.

1. Stay in shape. Make sure you eat well and get plenty of exercise. Not only do you want to look good in your uniform, but, more importantly, you want to appear to effortlessly carry guests' baggage, and certainly without straining or hurting yourself, although you should use a luggage cart wherever feasible.

2. Look impeccable. Go above and beyond what is expected and look your best. Make sure your uniform is always neatly pressed, your shoes perfectly shined and your hair neat and in its place.

3. Know the hotel and its rooms inside and out. Learn all you can about the amenities and features so that you can knowledgeably respond when guests ask you about them. And they will.

4. Go out of your way to help guests. If a guest asks you how to use the DVD player in his room or get tickets to the big show in town, then show him. But if you don't know how to help the guest with his request, then gracefully go get someone who can.

5. Smile, be pleasant and have a positive, professional attitude. Your job is to help guests have a pleasant stay; this includes assisting them with their baggage, of course, but this extends to treating guests in a warm, professional and respectful manner that will make them want to come back and stay at the hotel again and again.

6. Anticipate guests' needs. Don't wait for guests to struggle with the weight of their bags and then look around for a bellman. Offer to help any guest or potential guest you see arriving or departing with a bag.

7. Always heed the instructions of your bell captain (your boss) and be available when you are needed. He should know where you are and how to get in touch with you. Your bell captain will assign you tasks, as appropriate.

课文 2 Text B

Section Ⅰ: Dialog

Interpret the following dialog alternatively into English and Chinese.

客人: Hello. I'm ready to check out. Could you pick up my luggage, please?
行李员: 当然，夫人。请问，您的房间号码是什么？ 好的，我马上上去。
行李员: Hello. Luggage service, ma'am.
客人: 噢，请进。
行李员: Are you all packed, ma'am?
客人: 是的，都打好了。
行李员: Is this all the luggage you have here, ma'am? Three suitcases?
客人: 还有一个旅行包，在桌子底下。
行李员: I see. Let me put them into the luggage cart.

客人：好的。

行李员：Are you ready to leave now, ma'am?

客人：准备走了，先生。

行李员：You'd better take a second look around, ma'am. Be sure not to leave behind your personal belongings except your smiles.

客人：这是个不错的建议。

行李员：If you are sure you have everything, ma'am, shall we go now?

客人：噢，天啊，我差点忘了这个胸针。这是买给我姐姐的礼物。我昨晚放在桌子上了，不知道什么时候掉地上了。谢谢，小伙子。

行李员：You are welcome, ma'am. That's why people say "Better sure than sorry."

客人：没错。走吧。

行李员：We are lucky. The elevator is here.

客人：是的，真幸运。实际上，这是我住过的最好的酒店。我肯定，下次来还住这儿。肯定。

行李员：I'm glad to hear that, ma'am.

客人：我是当真的。嗯，到一楼了。

行李员：Watch your step, ma'am. And this way, please.

客人：好的。

行李员：After you are finished checking out, I'll see you to the shuttle bus to the airport.

客人：谢谢，小伙子。你帮了大忙。

行李员：At your service, ma'am.

客人：嗯，趁我还没忘，拿着这点钱，找个地方好好吃一顿。

行李员：Oh, thank you, ma'am. It's very kind of you.

客人：好人有好报。

行李员：Thank you. Go ahead, please, ma'am. The cashier is ready to check you out.

客人：好的，待会见。

行李员：In a while, crocodile.

Section Ⅱ: Passage

Interpret the following passage into Chinese.

The Core Competencies a Concierge Should Have for Duties

If you are a person who likes travel and tourism, working as a hotel concierge is a good way to provide helpful customer service while learning more about your town. Concierges make reservations and travel arrangements for guests. They are expected to know the hottest dining spots and how to get tickets to a sold-out show.

Navigation

A good concierge should have a sense of direction and knowledge of how to navigate the area on foot, by public transit and in a car. Most guests will not be familiar with the area and may rely on the concierge to get them to tourist attractions, major museums and even a place to get coffee or a newspaper in the morning. The concierge will usually have maps; she should provide the guests with the map and explain the route to them carefully.

Language

Not all travelers speak English, so hotels may prefer a concierge with good knowledge of another language, such as Spanish, German or Chinese. While language skills are not required, they may help a concierge earn more money. A concierge with language skills can assist other hotel personnel in helping foreign travelers with their needs.

Research Skills

Sometimes concierges may have to fulfill odd requests for travelers. In this case, a concierge needs to be able to find the relevant information and find it fast, especially if the patron is waiting. A concierge needs to know where to find this information, how to tell if a source is reliable and how to navigate the Internet, phone directory and guide books at his disposal.

Customer Service

Most of the concierge's job is spent talking to someone, either in person or over the phone. Accordingly, the best concierges love talking to people and helping people. For great customer service, she will need to network and make inroads at fine dining restaurants, popular tourist attractions, theater companies and other venues where clients like to go. A good concierge will be able to make spa and personal care appointments for hotel guests, send guests to great restaurants and secure impossible reservations, all while keeping a positive and upbeat attitude.

Section Ⅲ: Passage
Interpret the following passage into English.

代客泊车

泊车员负责在旅馆、餐馆和商店为客人泊车。一些机构会收取费用，而另一些机构则是免费的。泊车员通常受雇于某个机构,如酒店,或为代泊服务公司工作。他们的工资通常很低,但大都可以从客人那里得到小费。

车辆评估

泊车员在车抵达时负责评估,看看车体上是否有明显的损伤。他们需要对任何表面损伤进行登记,以免客户抱怨车况引起争端。

普通泊车

泊车员在泊车时要安全有效。泊车员应该把车停在所在酒店或餐厅指定的空间内。正如"都市泊车服务网站"上所说的,泊车记录上写明哪辆车停在哪个地方,每位客人都有一张泊车单。有些泊车员受雇于某些募捐活动,这些活动往往把某个地方包租一晚上。当受雇于这些场合时,泊车员需要在场地以外的地方泊车,如附近的街道上或多层停车场内。

优先停车

泊车员可能要根据雇主的要求把某些车辆停在某些位置。这在高档餐馆时有发生。在那里,高消费的客人都有预留车位,这样,他们就可以轻轻松松地到达,轻轻松松地离开。婚礼上也是如此,以示对尊贵客人的敬意。泊车员需要熟练掌控各种车辆。

车位调度和维护

泊车员应保持停车区域干净整洁,确保所有车辆有序停放。他们还要确保所有空间都得到充分利用。如果空间不足,应及时通知经理。

取车与存档

客人取回车辆时,泊车员要联系收银员。收银员妥善保存所有车辆钥匙和停车单据,直到客人离开。泊车员还负责记录自己当班时出现的任何事件、任何事故。

客户服务

泊车员在安排客人车辆停放时,要做到毕恭毕敬,周全周到。泊车员还要为客人打开车门,让客人上车。他们还负责回答大众有关当地景点和到达景点最快路径方面的问题。

Section Ⅰ : Dialog

客人:你好。我要离店了。请帮我把行李拿下去,好吗?

行李员:Sure, ma'am. May I have your room number, please? OK. I'll be right up.

行李员:您好,行李服务,夫人。

客人:Oh, come in, please.

行李员：您的行李都打好了吗，夫人？

客人：Yes, I am.

行李员：夫人，您所有的行李都在这儿吗？3个旅行箱？

客人：And a traveling bag under the table.

行李员：明白。让我把它们放到行李车里。

客人：OK.

行李员：准备走了吗，夫人？

客人：As ready as I can be, sir.

行李员：夫人，您最好再看一看，不要把您的私人物品落下，但请把您的微笑留下。

客人：That's good advice.

行李员：夫人，如果行李都齐了，我们走吧。

客人：Oh my, I almost forgot the brooch. It's a gift for my elder sister. I put it on the table last night. And I don't know when it fell to the floor. Thank you, young man.

行李员：不客气，夫人。要不人们怎么会说"稳当总比后悔强"呢。

客人：Exactly. Let's go now.

行李员：真幸运，电梯来了。

客人：Yes, we are. This is actually the nicest hotel I have ever stayed in. I'm sure I'll stay here next time I come. That's a promise.

行李员：您这么说，我很高兴，夫人。

客人：I am serious. Well, here we are at the first floor.

行李员：小心脚下，夫人。这边请。

客人：OK.

行李员：您办完离店手续之后，我送您去坐机场大巴。

客人：Thank you, young man. You have been a great help.

行李员：愿意为您效劳，夫人。

客人：Well, before I forget, take this money and have a dinner somewhere.

行李员：噢，谢谢，夫人。您真客气。

客人：Good things happen to good people.

行李员：谢谢。您去吧，夫人。收银员等着给您结账呢。

客人：OK. See you later, alligator.

行李员：待会见。

Section II: Passage

礼宾服务人员应具备的核心竞争力

如果你是一个喜欢旅游和旅游行业的人，那么，作酒店礼宾人员是一个很好的选择，可以为客户提供方便有用的服务，也可以深入了解自己所在的城市。礼宾人员为客人预订房间，安排旅程。他们应该知道哪儿是最受欢迎的就餐地点，如何在演出票销售一空的情况下设法弄到票。

导航能力

一个优秀的礼宾人员应该有方向感，知道当地的步行线路、公交线路和驾驶线路。大多数客人对当地并不熟悉，需要依赖礼宾人员给他们指路才能到达旅游景点、主要的博物馆，甚至是一大早找个喝咖啡的地方或买一份早报的地方。礼宾人员通常都有地图。他们应该给客人提供地图，仔细为客人讲解线路。

语言能力

不是所有的游客都会英语，所以，酒店更喜欢精通另一种语言的礼宾人员，如西班牙语、德语或汉语等。虽然酒店对礼宾人员没有语言方面的要求，但语言方面的技能会增加礼宾人员的收入。懂外语的礼宾人员可以协助酒店其他人员解决外国游客的需求。

研究能力

有时，礼宾人员需要满足客人奇怪的要求。在这种情况下，礼宾人员要能找到相关的信息，而且要快，尤其是客人就在一旁等待的时候。礼宾人员要知道去哪儿寻找相关信息，要能判断出消息来源是否可靠，要熟练浏览互联网、电话簿和导游指南等。

客服能力

礼宾人员的大部分工作是与客人交流，要么是面对面交流，要么是在电话里交流。因此，一流的礼宾人员喜欢与人交流，喜欢帮助别人。为更好地服务客人，礼宾人员需要建立关系网，"打入"高档餐厅、备受推崇的旅游景点、电影公司和其他客人喜欢光顾的地方。优秀的礼宾人员能为客人进行水疗、个人护理方面的预约，能把客人送到高档餐厅，能在几乎不可能的情况下为客人进行预订，而且，在整个过程中都能保持一种积极乐观的态度。

Section Ⅲ: Passage

Valet Parking

A valet parking attendant is responsible for parking cars at hotels, restaurants and stores. Some businesses charge a fee for the privilege of valet parking, whereas others offer it as a courtesy service. Valets are typically hired by an establishment, such as a hotel, or work for a valet services firm. They usually work for low salaries, but tips from customers are a common feature of the role.

Vehicle Assessment

Valets are responsible for assessing every vehicle upon arrival to check whether there is any damage visible on the bodywork. They are required to document any surface damage to avoid disputes should a customer complain about a vehicle's condition.

General Parking

A valet attendant should operate each vehicle safely and efficiently when parking it. Valets are expected to park vehicles within the designated spaces attached to the hotel or restaurant where they are employed. As stated on the Metropolitan Parking Services website, a valet record records which car has been parked in which space and each customer is provided with a valet ticket. Some valets are hired for fund-raising events held at venues that are booked for a single night. When employed on these occasions, valets may have to park cars at an off-site location, on streets nearby or at a multi-story car park.

Priority Parking

Valet attendants may be required to park certain vehicles in certain spaces, according to the instructions of the employer. This may occur in expensive restaurants, where high-spending guests are given priority spaces so they can arrive and leave in comfort, or at weddings to respect the hierarchy of important visitors. A valet attendant should be adept at safely handling a range of vehicle types.

Parking Space Scheduling and Maintenance

Valet attendants are expected to keep parking areas clean and ensure all vehicles are parked in an orderly fashion. They should also ensure that all available spaces are maximized and inform their managers should there be a shortage of spaces.

Vehicle Retrieval and Documentation

Valets contact the valet cashier when a customer asks for their vehicle back. Valet cashiers securely store all vehicle keys and parking tickets until a customer is ready to leave. Valet attendants are also responsible for documenting any incidents and accidents that occur during their shifts.

Customer Service

Valets should be courteous and considerate when arranging for customers' cars to be parked. Valets also open car doors to allow customers to enter vehicles. They are also expected to field any inquiries from the public regarding local attractions and the fastest routes to reach them.

第3单元
办理入住

Reception and Check-in

课文 1   Text A

Section Ⅰ: Dialog
Interpret the following dialog alternatively into English and Chinese.

前台：Good evening, sir. Welcome to Hyatt Hotel. Can I help you?

客人：我刚打过电话。我要办理入住手续。

前台：Could you please tell me your name, sir?

客人：比尔·琼斯。

前台：Just a second, Mr. Jones. Let me check. ... Yes, you called half an hour ago, and you booked a suite, a deluxe suite for tonight. Am I right?

客人：对，小姐。

前台：May I see your passport, please?

客人：给。

前台：And your credit card?

客人：给。

前台：Fill out this registration card, please, and be sure to sign your name on the dotted line.

客人：好的。

前台：How long will you be staying here?

客人：我星期五上午离开。

前台：OK, Mr. Jones, your room number is 8216.

客人：8216? 八楼？ 我记得我说过，我想住在低一点的楼层。

前台：No, sir. It's on the second floor.

客人：那为什么是 8216？

前台：Oh, it's a standard practice to put the number 8 before the number of a hotel room in China. For 8 is a lucky number in Chinese folk culture. It is pronounced the same as another word fa, meaning rich.

客人：有意思。

前台：It sure is. Now, Mr. Jones, the bellboy will show you to your room. I wish you a pleasant stay here.

客人：谢谢，小姐。晚安。

前台：One more thing, Mr. Jones. Breakfast is from 7 to 9. The dining room is on the third floor.

客人：谢谢。

前台：Have a great night.

Section II: Passage
Interpret the following passage into Chinese.

Ten Commandments of Front Desk Clerks

The front desk is typically where customers develop their first impression of a business. A bad first impression is often difficult to change, so offering exemplary customer service is a must for front desk clerks. One of the most valuable assets a business has is its repeat customers; by ensuring a pleasant front desk experience, business owners are making an investment into their own future.

1. The Customer is Always Right

The customers' needs and concerns should come first. When customers approach the front desk, focus attention on them.

2. Practice Active Listening

The only way to clearly identify customers' needs is to hear them out. A customer should not be interrupted when speaking. If you do not understand what a customer is saying, allow him to finish speaking before asking for clarification.

3. Anticipate Customers' Needs

When a customer approaches the front desk, try to silently anticipate his needs. If there is additional information that can be shared to assist with a need, work to provide that.

4. Make Every Customer Feel Valued

People do business where they feel most comfortable. A bad experience with a previous customer should not affect the next client's experience. Treat customers as individuals and make them feel special by remembering their names or any other information that will exemplify their value to the business.

5. Help Customers Understand Your Process

Customers are not behind the scenes and often have no idea what your business policies are. Work to inform customers of your process with clarity and tact.

6. Make Helping the Priority

Customers appreciate the power of yes. Always look for ways to help clients. Make it easy for them to do business with the company.

7. Keep Your Cool

In a perfect world, all customers would be pleasant. This is far from the case, and the front desk is where most complaints land. If the customer appears to be getting angry, work to calm him down. Do not argue or challenge customers. Call a senior team member if the situation escalates beyond what is safe and appropriate.

8. Exceed Customer Expectations

Happy customers help build successful businesses. Customers who are pleased with their front desk experiences will be more likely to return. By offering customers something they were not expecting, you are contributing to an overall pleasant experience.

9. Maintain a Neat and Professional Experience

Customers may make determinations about the business based solely on their experience at the front desk. Front desk personnel and their seating areas should be neat and orderly at all times.

10. Encourage Feedback

Allow customers the opportunity to give feedback on their experiences. They may have suggestions that could benefit the front desk environment or the business as a whole.

Section Ⅲ: Passage
Interpret the following passage into English.

前台接待员应具备的素质

酒店的前台工作可以说是开启酒店管理事业的一个很好的方式。然而，这也是一个压力很大、有时甚至是令人厌恶的工作。只要你有足够的耐心和不凡的能力，这份工作也可能带你走进一个非常充实的职业生涯。以下是在酒店前台工作应具备的素质。

1. 苦练打字本领

大多数酒店会要求你能在一分钟打很多字。你可以通过几个不同的网站在线测试你的打字能力。为了能在酒店前台工作，你每分钟的输入速度应该在60到80个单词之间。确切的输入速度取决于你工作的酒店。

2. 增强你的计算机应用能力

大多数酒店都有一个特定的软件，用于办理客人入住和离店结账手续。你极有可能不熟悉该程序中的每一个工具，除非以前在酒店工作过。不过，你应该精通文字处理程序和电子表格程序。面试时，面试官可能会测试你对上述程序的熟练程度。你无须利用这些程序处理复杂的文件，但你应掌握基础的技能。如果你在中学、技校或者大学选修了类似课程，那么，你完全能胜任酒店的前台工作。

3. 能同时胜任多项工作

毫无疑问，在酒店前台工作，有时需要同时处理很多任务。例如，你可能需要一边打电话，一边在电脑上查看是否有房间，然后，给客人办理入住手续。重要的是，你在同时处理所有任务时，不出任何差错。

4. 面试时，做到举止优雅，信心满满

在酒店前台工作，需要具备人际交往的很多技能。一天之内，你会遇到各种各样的人，其中一些很难打交道。重要的是，在善待每位客人的前提下，不要做出过多的让步。如果你在面试时能展示这方面的特长，录用的可能性就会大大增加。

5. 要有耐心，要很有耐心

如果你在一家高档酒店前台工作，这一点尤为重要。不幸的是，在这些场所出现的客人大都觉得他们比你"强"，或者说，至少会以这样的态度对待你。在这些人面前，你显然不能抬高自己的声音。也有一些人，目的就是想在房费上打个折扣，这些人办理离店手续时会到处找茬。重要的是，你要仔细处理每一种情况，要有良好的态度。在酒店前台工作意味着，在客人面前你就是公司的脸面，哪怕仅有几分钟的时间。你总是希望客人离开时感到自己得到了最好的服务，这样，他们将来还会再来。

参考答案

Section Ⅰ： Dialog

前台：先生，晚上好。欢迎来到凯悦酒店。有什么能为您效劳吗？

客人：Yes. I just called. I'd like to check in, please.

前台：先生，请问您的姓名？

客人：Bill Jones.

前台：请稍等，琼斯先生。我查查。…… 对，您半小时前打来电话，您订了一个套间，一个豪华套间。今晚入住，对吧？

客人：You are right, young lady.

前台：请给我您的护照。

客人：Here it is.

前台：还有您的信用卡。

客人：Here you are.

前台：请填写这张登记卡，别忘了在虚线上签名。

客人：All right.

前台：您打算住多久？

客人：I'll be leaving Friday morning.

前台：好的，琼斯先生，您的房间号是8216。

客人：8216? Is it on the eighth floor? I remember I told you that I prefer to stay on the lower levels.

前台：不是，先生。您的房间在2楼。

客人：Then, why 8216?

前台：噢，在中国，习惯在房间号码前加上数字8，因为8在中国民间文化中是个吉祥的数字。8和"发"谐音，是"发财"的意思。

客人：That's interesting.

前台：是的。好了，琼斯先生，行李员现在送您去房间。祝您在此过得愉快。

客人：Thank you, miss. Good night.

前台：还有一件事，琼斯先生，早餐时间是7点到9点。餐厅在3楼。

客人：Thank you.

前台：祝您度过一个愉快的夜晚。

Section II : Passage

前台服务十诫

一般来说，前台是客户对一个公司产生第一印象的地方。第一印象一旦不好，很难改变。因此，对前台服务员来说，为客人提供优质服务是一个不可或缺的条件。公司最有价值的资产之一是它的回头客。企业老板通过提供一个愉快的前台经历为自己投资未来。

1. 顾客永远是正确的

客户的需求和关注点应该是第一位的。当客人走到前台时，要把所有注意力都放在他们身上。

2. 学会积极倾听

要想弄清客户的需求，唯一的方法是听他们把话说完。客户说话的时候，不能打断。如果你没弄清楚客户的意思，先让他说完，然后再让他澄清。

3. 预测客户的需求

当客户走近前台时，设法悄悄预测他的需求。如果有额外的信息可以共享以满足客人需求，那就主动提供吧。

4. 让每一位客户感受自己很重要

做生意的前提是感到舒适愉快。与前一个客户之间糟糕的经历不应该影响到下一个客户。把客户当作个人来看待，记住他们的名字或任何能体现他们价值的信息，让每个人都感到自己很特别。

5. 帮助客户了解你工作的流程

客户不了解内情，常常不知道你的经营方针是什么。要用巧妙的方式把你的工作流程清清楚楚告诉客户。

6. 帮助客人永远是第一位的

客户都喜欢受到赏识。要想方设法帮助客户，使之可以轻轻松松地与公司做生意。

7. 保持冷静

在理想世界里，所有客户都是讨人喜欢的。事实远非如此，而且，前台是投诉最集中的地方。如果客户看上去要生气了，努力使他平静下来。不要和客户理论，更不要挑战客户。如果事态升级，超出安全范围，赶快找一个资深同事来救场。

8. 超越顾客期望

顾客高兴了，企业就成功了。对前台服务很满意的顾客往往会成为回头客。给客户提供一些他们意想不到的东西，会使他们的经历变得更加愉快。

9. 永远提供整洁专业的体验

客户业务方面的决定可能完全基于他们在前台的经历。因此，前台工作人员及其座位区必须永远保持整洁有序。

10. 鼓励反馈意见

给顾客提供一个机会，让他们就自己的经历提出反馈意见。顾客可能会提出一些建议，对前台环境乃至整个企业环境都有好处。

Section Ⅲ: Passage

How to Work Front Desk at a Hotel

Working at the front desk of a hotel can be an excellent way to begin a career in hotel management. However, this can also be a very stressful and at times annoying job. With the right amount of patience and skills, this could be a job that catapults you into a very fulfilling career. Here is how to work front desk at a hotel.

1. Work on your typing skills

Most hotels will require you to have the ability to type so many words a minute. You can test your typing skills online through several different websites. In order to work front desk at a hotel, you should be able to type somewhere between 60 and 80 words per minute. The exact number will depend on the hotel where you work.

2. Expand on your computer skills

Most hotels have a specific software program used for checking in and billing guests. Chances are that you will not know how to use every tool of this program unless you've worked in a hotel before. However, you should be knowledgeable in both word processing programs and spreadsheet programs. The hotel you are interviewing with may even test you on your competency in these two programs. You won't have to perform large tasks with these programs but you should know the basics. If you've taken any class in high school, vocational school or college regarding these two programs, you will be more than prepared to work front desk at a hotel.

3. Be able to do multi-task

There will unquestionably come a time while working front desk at a hotel when you will have to perform a couple of tasks at the same time. For example, you may have to be on the phone while checking the computer to see if a room is available and then checking that person in. It's important that you can handle all of these tasks without making any mistakes.

4. Be personable yet confident during your interview

You need plenty of people skills to work front desk at a hotel. You will encounter a variety of people throughout your day and some will be difficult. It's important that you can be friendly with these people, all the while not giving in too much. If you can show these characteristics during the interview process, you will increase the likelihood of getting hired.

5. Have patience and lots of it

This is especially important if you are working front desk at an upscale hotel. Unfortunately, many of the guests at these establishments will believe that they are "better" than you (or at least that is how you will be treated). You obviously cannot raise your voice to these individuals. There are also people out there who are simply looking to get a deal on their hotel room. These people may decide to come up with "complaints" while checking out. It's important that you handle every situation carefully and with a good attitude. Working front desk at a hotel means that you are the face of the company to guests, even if only for a few minutes. You want the guests to always leave feeling that they received the best service possible so that they will return for another stay.

课文2 Text B

Section I: Dialog
Interpret the following dialog alternatively into English and Chinese.

客人：Hello, miss.
前台：先生，您好。有什么能为您效劳的吗？
客人：I'd like to check in, please.

前台：先生，您预约了吗？

客人：My friend Robert Dickinson made it for me 2 days ago.

前台：请稍等。恐怕找不到以这个名字所做的预约记录。

客人：That's impossible.

前台：我再查查。先生，请说一下您的名字。

客人：Jack Johnson.

前台：不好意思，约翰逊先生，我们没有罗伯特·迪金森以您的名义所做的预约记录。

客人：Do you have any vacancies?

前台：先生，您想要什么样的房间？单人间，双人间，还是……?

客人：A single room is preferable. I'd like a quiet room, away from the street, if possible. And it would be much better if it is one with a view.

前台：带景致的房间。嗯，先生，只有三个单人间了，一个对着山，一个对着游泳池，还有一个对着停车场。

客人：A parking lot? I think you are pulling my leg. Well, in that case, I'll settle for the first one.

前台：好的。

客人：What are your rates?

前台：每晚488元。

客人：What services come with that?

前台：三星级酒店的服务设施都有，比如国内直拨、国际直拨、卫星电视、宽带上网，还有一个小酒吧。

客人：Do you have a complimentary breakfast?

前台：是的。先生，您现在可以办理入住手续了吗？

客人：Yes, I'm ready.

前台：好的。请出示您的护照、信用卡，并在这张登记卡上签名。

客人：Here you are.

前台：这是您的房间钥匙。去那边坐电梯，到三楼，走到走廊的尽头，往右拐。您的房间就在眼前。

客人：Thank you.

前台：再见。

Section Ⅱ：Passage

Interpret the following passage into Chinese.

The Do's & Don'ts of Telephone Etiquette

If you work at the front desk of a hotel, focus on telephone etiquette.

Knowing what to do and what not to do when answering and speaking on the phone is imperative. It will help you to acquire and retain clients.

Do Speak Clearly

Make sure that all your words are clear when you speak to the caller. Enunciate your words while slightly smiling. Speak slowly; the person on the other end of the phone conversation needs to understand you.

Do Greet Customers Appropriately

When you answer the phone, greet the customer according to the time of day (e. g. "good morning", "good afternoon", "good evening"). Thank the customer for calling—this invites the customer to feel comfortable voicing a complaint or asking a question.

Do Ask How You Can Help

Ask the customer how you can be of service when greeting them. After listening to the customer's reason for calling—and you can't be of assistance—attempt to transfer the consumer to the appropriate department.

Do Listen to the Caller's Request

Listen carefully to the caller's request. Ask the customer applicable questions to determine how you can help. Don't interrupt when the caller is speaking.

Do Ask to Place the Caller on Hold

Before you place a caller on hold, ask permission first. Once you've pressed the hold button, quickly work to address the customer's problem as quickly as possible.

Don't Talk with Your Mouth Full

Don't pick up the phone with your mouth full. This makes it difficult for the caller to understand you—and is frustrating—especially if the call is urgent. Answering the phone at work while eating gives an unprofessional impression.

Don't Speak too Loudly or Softly

Answer the phone in the volume that you normally speak. Speaking softly will make it challenging for the caller to understand what you're saying. Talking softly may confuse the caller, unsure that he has dialed the right number. Answering the phone too loudly sounds harsh and abrasive, which is an unappealing to the caller.

Don't Leave the Caller on Hold

If you have to place the caller on hold, don't leave the person calling on hold for a long period of time. Check back every few seconds to keep the caller informed on your progress.

Don't Use Slang Words

Using slang or shortened words during phone conversation is inappropriate and unprofessional. For instance, if you have to check on something for the customer, say "just a moment", not "hold on a sec".

Don't Answer the Phone Casually

Instead of simply saying "hello" when answering a business phone, state the name of the hotel or state the hotel's slogan immediately.

Section Ⅲ: Passage
Interpret the following passage into English.

前台接待员注意事项

一个态度和蔼、快乐高效的接待员是企业的重要财富。接待员象征着公司的原则，体现了对客户的尊重、对客户的价值。真诚二字对接待员来说极为重要。公司团队中有一个精明能干的接待员，能给客户留下非常难忘的第一印象。如果你想成为成功的接待员，下面这几点建议非常实用。

积极倾听

作为一名接待员，你要经常与人打交道。你要面对的是满口怨言的客户、焦躁不安的经理和其他一些想要倾诉的人。因此，积极倾听的技巧至关重要。你需要一双敏锐的耳朵，捕捉对方用言语表达的信息和通过肢体语言表达出来的信息。要全神贯注地听，不要让噪音、周围的人或其他事情分散你的注意力。要有耐心，不要催促对方或打断对方。等对方说完，再去提问题。如果你是在捎口信，重复给对方听听，以确保没有记错。

遵守电话礼仪

遵守电话礼仪是接待员的基本技能。要用欢快的语调问候来电的人。对方说话的时候，要认真去听；你回话时，要口齿清晰。不要直呼对方的名字。即便对方很令人恼火，也要有耐心。打电话的过程中，如果需要处理另一个来电，或者为对方核实相关信息，要征得对方同意，不可直接把对方晾在一边。如果是你打给别人，要先告诉对方你是何许人也，然后再切入主题。说话时，要清晰简洁，节省对方的时间，提高自己的工作效率。

做公司的销售代理

尽管这不是接待员职责的一部分，但如果你可以创造销售机会，那么，你就可以为公司创造价值。一个叫作"好客世界网络"的网站举了这么一个例子，很好地诠释了这一概念。它说，酒店前台接待员在散客询问房价时往往只说出房价，如"每晚100美元"。这样的回答既不能帮助客人作出决定，也不能帮助酒店招揽生意。相反，接待员应该向客人解释房间信息及相关服务。最好向客人说明酒店有哪些不同的选择，有哪些配套服务，这会让游客停住脚步，思考一番，作出决定。

客户服务

与人打交道的能力，对一个旨在为客人提供良好服务的接待员来说，至关重要。要设身处地地为客户着想，及时消除他们的怨气。"好客世界网络"提供了一个很好的例子，说明糟糕的前台服务能带来什么恶果。它说，一个外地游客想要了解一下本地最好的景点，来到了前台，对方却给了他一张地图。可是，地图网上都有啊。作为本地人，前台应该做的是提供一些有价值的建议，这才是客户真正期待的。

参考答案

Section Ⅰ: Dialog

客人：小姐，你好。

前台：Hello, sir. What can I do for you?

客人：我想办理入住手续。

前台：Do you have a reservation with us, sir?

客人：我朋友罗伯特·迪金森两天前为我预约的。

前台：Wait a minute, please. I'm afraid we have no reservation by this name.

客人：不可能。

前台：Let me have a check again. Your name, please, sir?

客人：杰克·约翰逊。

前台：Sorry, Mr. Johnson, we have no record of any reservation made in your name by Robert Dickinson.

客人：还有空房间吗？

前台：What kind of room would you like, sir? A single room, a double room, or...?

客人：最好是单人间。如果可能，我想要一个安静的房间，远离马路。带景致就更好了。

前台：One with a view. Well, we only have three single rooms left, sir, one with a view of a hill, one, of a swimming pool, and one, of a parking lot.

客人：停车场？ 我想您是在开玩笑吧。嗯，那样的话，还是第一个吧。

前台：OK.

客人：房费是多少？

前台：488 yuan per night.

客人：都有什么服务设施？

前台：It has the usual collection of services required of a 3-star hotel, such as DDD, IDD, a satellite TV, broadband internet connections, and a mini-bar.

客人：早餐免费吗？

前台：Yes, we do. Are you ready to check in, sir?

客人：可以。

前台：Good. We need your passport, credit card and your signature in this registration form.

客人：给。

前台：Here's your key. Take the elevator over there to the third floor, go down to the end of the corridor and turn right. You will find your room right in front of you.

客人：谢谢。

前台：Cheerio.

Section Ⅱ：Passage

电话礼仪五要五不要

如果你在酒店前台工作，一定要注意电话礼仪。知道接电话或打电话时该做什么不该做什么十分必要，它有助于你获得客户并留住客户。

口齿要清楚

务必确保你说的每一个字对方都听得清清楚楚。说话时，要面带笑容。语速不要太快，让电话另一端的人能够听懂。

打招呼时要得体

接电话时，根据一天中的不同时间段来问候客户，如"早上好""下午好""晚上好"。谢谢客户打来电话，这会使前来投诉或提问题的客户感到自在一些。

询问能为对方提供什么帮助

问候客户时，顺便问一下能为对方提供什么服务。获知对方打来电话的原因之后，如果你无法提供帮助，就要把对方的电话转到相应部门。

聆听对方的请求

仔细聆听对方的请求。问客户一些相关的问题，以确定你能提供什么帮助。对方说话时，不要打断。

让客户在线上等候时一定要先征求对方的意见

让客户在线上等候之前，一定要先征得对方的同意。一旦按下"等候"键，就要尽快找出解决问题的方法。

嘴里有东西时不要说话

嘴里有食物时,不要拿起电话,因为对方很难听懂,而且会让人十分恼火,尤其是在有急事的情况下。接电话时吃东西会给人留下很不专业的印象。

说话时声音不能过大,也不能过小

接电话时,声音大小要正常。声音过小,对方很难听懂,会让对方感到困惑,不知道自己是否拨对了号码。声音过大,听起来很刺耳,很粗暴,令人生厌。

不要把对方晾在一边

如果你不得不让客户在线上等候,不要让对方等太长时间。每隔几秒钟回来,告诉对方进展情况。

不要使用俚语

打电话时使用俚语或缩略词既不合适,也不专业。例如,如果你为客户核实什么不得不暂时中断电话时,要说 Just a moment,而不要说 Hold on a sec.

接电话时不要太随便

接电话时,不要仅仅说一声"您好"就完事了,而要马上加上酒店的名称或者酒店的标语。

Section Ⅲ: Passage

Tips for Front Desk Receptionists

A warm, cheerful and efficient receptionist is an important asset for a business. A receptionist symbolizes the company's principles and its respect and value for its customers. Sincerity in approach is very important for a receptionist. With a competent receptionist on its team, a company can be sure of creating a memorable first impression on clients. If you are looking to make it as a successful receptionist, some tips can be handy.

Listen Actively

In the role of a receptionist, you interact with people a lot. You have complaining customers, anxious managers and other people who want you to listen. As such, active listening skills are crucial. You need a keen ear to listen to the speaker's vocalized message and his non-vocalized message conveyed through his body language. Give rapt attention to what the speaker is saying without letting noise, people or other surrounding things distract you. Be patient and do not hurry or interrupt the speaker. Wait until she has finished and then pose questions if any. If you are taking a message, repeat it to the giver to ensure that you have got it correctly.

Observe Telephone Manners

Telephone etiquette is an essential skill for receptionists. Greet callers with a cheerful tone. Listen to them as they talk, and reply clearly. Address callers with their surnames. Try to be patient even if the caller is irritating. While on a call, if you need to handle another incoming call or check for information relevant to the caller, seek permission first instead of straight away asking the caller to hold on. If it is you calling someone, inform them who you are and then proceed to give the message. Be clear and concise in your speech to save time for the listener and get your work done quickly.

Be Your Company's Selling Agent

Though this is not part of your receptionist responsibilities, you can add value to your company by creating selling opportunities. An example that Hospitality World Network website gives in this regard explains this concept better: Front desk receptionists in hotels often respond to inquiries from walk-in visitors on room cost with just the price, "It's $100 for a night stay." This in no way helps the visitor make a decision or the hotel get business. Instead, receptionists should explain visitors along with the room rent information, the services they would be getting. Even better would be to explain different stay options and accompanying services available at the hotel, which would make visitors stop, think and make a decision.

Customer Service

The quality of being able to get along with people is vital for a receptionist to provide good customer service. Be empathetic to your customers' situation and address their grievances promptly. Hospitality World Network website provides a good example of bad customer service by the front desk: A nonlocal visitor who wanted some best advice on local attractions approached the front desk and was presented with a map. You can get maps on the Internet. What the front desk could have done is to offer some valuable suggestions on attractions as an area local, which was what the customer was expecting.

第4单元
送餐服务

Room Service

Text A

Section Ⅰ: Dialog
Interpret the following dialog alternatively into English and Chinese.

客人：Hello. Is that room service?

服务员：是的。有什么能为您效劳的吗，夫人？

客人：Can I have my lunch brought to the room?

服务员：当然，夫人。请告诉我您的姓名和房间号。

客人：Yes. This is Janet Jackson in Room 618.

服务员：夫人，您想吃点儿什么？

客人：Two beefsteaks, and two fried eggs.

服务员：牛排要几分熟的？

客人：One for medium well, and one for blue rare.

服务员：鸡蛋要老一点的还是嫩一点的？

客人：One for sunny side up, and one for sunny side down.

服务员：好的。还要点儿别的吗？比如说，沙拉？

客人：Oh yes. What would you recommend?

服务员：玫瑰花瓣沙拉，夫人。那是我们的特色菜，很特别。

客人：Good. I'll take it. And...

服务员：夫人，您想喝点什么？

客人：Two cups of coffee, please.

服务员：加不加牛奶，夫人？

客人：Without milk, please.

服务员：好的。就这么多吗，夫人？

客人：Yes, that's all. Thank you.

服务员：好的，夫人。两份牛排，一份七分熟的，一份一分熟的；两个煎蛋，一份嫩一点的，一份老一点的；一份玫瑰花瓣沙拉；两杯咖啡，不加牛奶。对吗，夫人？

客人：Yes, 100% correct. Well, when can I have them sent up to my room?

服务员：马上送过去。

客人：Thank you.

服务员：愿意为您效劳，夫人。

Section II: Passage
Interpret the following passage into Chinese.

The Food and Beverage Hospitality Points of Westin (Part One)

Our primary concern is to provide exemplary and consistent service to all of our food and beverage guests. The following Food and Beverage Hospitality Points have been developed to guide you in offering the best possible service in our food and beverage outlets.

Serving Our Guests-Our First and Last Impression

The most important element of your job is to make every guest feel important, welcomed and valued by projecting a genuine warmth and friendliness. Your duties should never detract from your efforts to make a positive lasting impression on all our guests.

Greet all guests with a smile and a positive attitude that says, "Welcome, we are happy you're here."

Smile, make eye contact and engage in pleasant but brief conversation.

Never allow a guest to leave dissatisfied.

Maintaining Professionalism

Projecting a positive and professional attitude is vital to providing exemplary service to our guests. This includes the manner in which we conduct ourselves as well as how we interact with our guests and our fellow associates.

Generally:

Always remain friendly and professional.

Always smile and make eye contact.

Do not chew gum, eat or drink anything while in public areas.

Do not speak louder than is necessary; maintain a quiet atmosphere for the guests.

Always stand with a straight posture; never lean or slouch.

Keep your hands at your sides and never have your arms folded or hands in your pockets.

With Guests:

Always be courteous and give the right-of-way.

Always strive to ensure that your guests' expectations have been exceeded.

Always use a guest's name whenever possible.

Never stand with your back to a guest.

Do not speak to your guests in a foreign language unless the guest initiates the conversation or cannot speak English (or the local language).

With Associates:

Never carry on conversations with fellow associates in a foreign language.

Never make derogatory remarks about your guests or fellow associates.

Never conduct personal conversations in the presence of guests.

Do not stand in groups in public areas.

Section Ⅲ: Passage

Interpret the following passage into English.

如何提高顾客餐饮满意度

提高顾客的餐饮满意度,方法很多。关键是,要确保所有客人都有一个愉快的经历。餐厅的客人希望服务员、收银员和餐厅主管都能态度和蔼,都能提供帮助。因此,要确保员工富有热情,并且热爱餐厅工作。客人还希望你能履行你在互联网、广播或广告黄页上许下的诺言。因此,要千方百计去满足甚至超越客人的期望。

首先,注重最基本的东西。

要想提高客人对你餐厅的满意度,其中一个方法是把重点放在基本的东西上。了解客人最关心的事情,质量、服务、清洁状况通常是大多数餐馆的关键变量。顾客希望吃到热气腾腾、美味可口的食物,并且,材质要好。有特殊需求的客人希望他们的菜单能得到相应的反映。例如,一位客人可能只想点烤鸡,不想要面包。那么,就为他提供他想要的好了。客人也希望服务员能时不时过来看看,时不时为他们续杯饮料。带孩子的客人可能需要儿童座椅或者高脚椅子。大部分客人希望就餐的地方窗明几净。这无疑会增加餐厅的吸引力。

其次,进行员工培训。

也可以通过对经理和员工进行良好培训来提高客服质量。大厨或其他准备饭菜的员工要知道烹调肉类需要多长时间,烹调蔬菜和其他食品又需要多长时间。同样,那些在快餐店工作的服务员应该了解菜单上每一种食物的正确分量。分量不足,客人会发现的。如果食物火候不到或者配料不足,就无法满足客人的期望。此外,要对员工进行卫生方面的培训,包括端菜上饭前一定要洗手等。

再次,及时更新菜品制作状态。

最好让客人知道他们所点的菜肴的状态。告诉客人,为什么他所点的菜需要花更长的时间。例如,客人可能点了一份较厚的牛排,自然需要更多的时间来准备。让客人知道,为什么点的菜延迟了。同时,如果点的菜需要很长时间准备,最好为客人提供一份免费甜点。千万不要让客人离开时留下对食物或服务不满的印象。

最后，对服务质量进行跟踪调查。

在酒店里，确保客人满意度的最好方法之一，是对自己的服务进行跟踪调查。要想做到这一点，最简单的方式是走到客人面前，询问一下他们对食物和服务是否满意。帮助那些有问题或想投诉的客人。告诉客人，你欢迎他们的光临，并邀请他们下次再来。跟踪调查的另一种方法是通过客户问卷调查。邀请餐厅客人填写调查表格，在饭菜质量、接待、服务和清洁等关键变量方面为你打分。通过开放式问题或者填空题，让客人详细说明他们的反应。然后，利用顾客反馈信息，提高餐馆业务水平。

Section Ⅰ：Dialog

客人：你好。请问，是送餐服务吗？

服务员：Yes. Can I help you, ma'am?

客人：可以把午餐送到我房间里来吗？

服务员：Certainly, ma'am. Would you give me your name and room number?

客人：好的。我叫珍妮特·杰克逊。房间号是618。

服务员：What would you like to have, ma'am?

客人：两份牛排，两个煎蛋。

服务员：How would you like your steaks served?

客人：一份七分熟，一份一分熟。

服务员：And how would you like your eggs done?

客人：一个嫩一点的，一个老一点的。

服务员：OK. Anything else? Say, a salad?

客人：要。你们这里有什么特色沙拉？

服务员：Rose-petal salad, ma'am. That's our signature dish. It's very special.

客人：好的，来一份。嗯，……

服务员：And what would you like to drink, ma'am?

客人：两杯咖啡。

服务员：With or without milk, ma'am?

客人：不加牛奶。

服务员：Good. Is that all, ma'am?

客人：对，就这么多。谢谢。

服务员：OK, ma'am. Two beefsteaks, one for medium well, and one for blue rare; two fried eggs, one for sunny side up, and one for sunny side down; a rose-petal salad, and two cups of coffee without milk. Am I correct, ma'am?

客人：对，100%正确。嗯，什么时候能送上来？

服务员：We will bright them up right away.

客人：谢谢。

服务员：At your service, ma'am.

Section Ⅱ：Passage

威斯汀餐饮服务条例（第一部分）

我们的主要目标是为客人提供持续优质的餐饮服务。下列"餐饮招待注意事项"旨在为在我店餐饮部门工作的人员提供指导，使之能为客人提供最优质的服务。

服务客人——我们的第一印象和最后印象

你工作中最重要的元素，是通过发自内心的真诚和友好让每一位客人感到自己很重要，很受欢迎，很受重视。你的责任就是集中精力，全心全意，给所有客人留下一个积极持久的印象。

带着微笑、带着积极的态度去迎接每一位客人，让人有这样的感觉："欢迎，在这里见到您，我们很高兴。"

保持微笑，与客人保持眼神接触，进行简短而愉快的交流。

永远不要让一位客人失意而去。

保持专业精神

积极、专业的态度至关重要，它是我们为客人提供优质服务的前提。这包括我们的行为方式以及我们与客人、与同事打交道的方式。

一般而言：

永远保持友好、专业的态度。

永远保持微笑，永远保持眼神交流。

不在公共场所嚼口香糖、吃东西或喝东西。

不大声喧哗，为客人提供一个安静的环境。

站有站相，不弯腰驼背，不左歪右斜。

双手自然下垂，不双臂交叉，不把手放在口袋里。

对客人：

永远毕恭毕敬，礼让他人。

永远力争超越客人的期望。

如果可能的话，总是称呼客人的名字。
永远不要背对客人。
不要用外语和客人交谈，除非客人主动如此，或者客人不懂英语或当地的语言。
对同事：
永远不和同事用外语交流。
永远不要贬损客人或同事。
永远不在客人面前进行私人交谈。
永远不要在公共场所站成一堆。

Section Ⅲ：Passage

How to Improve Guest Satisfaction in the Restaurant Industry

There are a number of ways to improve guest satisfaction in the restaurant industry. The key is making sure all guests have a pleasant experience. Restaurant customers like waiters, cashiers and hosts that are helpful and friendly. Therefore, make sure you hire enthusiastic employees who enjoy working at your restaurant. Customers also expect you to deliver what you promised in your Internet, radio or yellow pages advertising. Hence, strive to meet and even exceed your guests' expectations.

First, focus on the basics.

One way to improve customer satisfaction in your restaurant is to focus on the basics. Know your customers' priorities. Quality, service and cleanliness are usually key variables in most restaurants. Customers expect hot, tasty food with the right textures. Those with special requests expect their orders to reflect it. For example, a customer may want to order just grilled chicken without the bread. Thus, provide that guest with exactly what he wants. Guests also expect waitresses to check on them occasionally and refill their drinks. People with kids may need booster seats or high chairs. And most restaurant patrons prefer eating in establishments with clean windows and dining areas. It undoubtedly adds to the appeal of the restaurant.

Second, train your staff.

You also can improve customer service by ensuring that your managers and employees are properly trained. Chefs or those who prepare meals should know how long to cook meats, vegetables and other food items. Similarly, those serving food in fast food restaurants, for example, should learn the proper food portions for all menu items. Your customers know when they are being shortchanged on food portions. The food won't meet their expectations if it is undercooked or includes too few ingredients. Also, train your staff on the proper sanitation procedures, including washing their hands before serving food.

Third, provide updates on orders.

It is always best to keep your customers apprised of their order status. Tell a customer why his order is taking longer. For example, a customer may have ordered a thicker steak that naturally takes longer to cook. Let the customer know exactly why the order is delayed. Also, offer a free dessert if the order takes an unreasonable amount of time. Never let a customer leave your restaurant upset about her food or the service.

Finally, track your performance.

One of the best ways to ensure guest satisfaction in restaurants is to track your performance. The easiest way to accomplish this is by walking around and asking guests about their food and service. Help guests that have concerns or complaints. Tell people you appreciate their business and invite them to come back. Another way to track performance is through guest surveys. Invite restaurant patrons to fill out survey forms, rating you on key variables such as quality, hospitality, service and cleanliness. Allow customers to elaborate on their responses with open-ended or fill-in-the-blank questions. Use the customer feedback to make improvements in your restaurant operations.

Text B

Section I: Dialog

Interpret the following dialog alternatively into English and Chinese.

服务员：Room service. May I come in?

客人：快请进。

服务员：Hello, ma'am. Here is your lunch. Beefsteaks, eggs, salad, and coffee.

客人：谢谢，先生。把它们放在桌子上好了。

服务员：OK. And here are the flowers and the birthday cake...

客人：什么？我没有订这些东西，先生。

服务员：I know. They are from our general manager. We learned from your registration card that today is your husband's birthday.

客人：噢，你们想得真周到，先生。我朋友跟我说，这是一家很特别的酒店，现在我知道原因了。请代我们向你们经理说声谢谢。我丈夫回来后会非常激动的。他5分钟后就回来。

服务员：Will do, ma'am.

客人：噢，这还有一张贺卡。上面写着："生日快乐，查尔斯·杰克逊先生。您真是75岁的常青树、不老松啊！愿您年年有今日，岁岁有今朝。"先生，我都不知道该怎么感谢你们了。你知道吗？

服务员：What?

客人：我们打算晚上庆祝呢。

服务员：So you will celebrate twice today?

客人：没错，先生。

服务员：Well, since today is a special day for you, I guess I'd better leave you alone.

客人：小伙子，你真是很体贴人啊。

服务员：Before I leave, ma'am, would you please sign the bill here?

客人：好的。

服务员：And be sure to put your name on the dotted line.

客人：好的。给。

服务员：Thank you. Please call us if you need anything else.

客人：我会的。

服务员：Enjoy your lunch, please. Goodbye.

客人：再见。

Section II: Passage
Interpret the following passage into Chinese.

The Food and Beverage Hospitality Points of Westin (Part Two)

Speaking With Guests

Every time you speak with a guest, you have the opportunity to create a positive impression of the Westin. Positive guest interaction increases guest satisfaction and loyalty as well as provides us with vital information we can use to improve our services.

Always use a positive tone that displays genuine concern.

Practice active listening. Active listening is the ability to focus your full attention on the current call or guest interaction and respond in an appropriate manner.

Maintain eye contact when speaking to guests.

Remain patient if asked to repeat or explain something again.

Always use the guest's name, if known.

When you do not know their name, use "Sir" or "Madam".

Whenever referring to the hotel or its F&B outlets, never use the terms "they", "them" and "theirs", always use "we", "us" and "ours".

Never inquire into the personal affairs of the guest.

Accurately answer all questions. If you do not know the answer, do not say, "I don't know." Instead, tell the guest that you will find out and go get the answer as quickly as possible. Never refer the guest to someone else. Never give inaccurate information. Go the extra mile!

The 10 and 5 Rule

When guests are within ten feet, smile, make eye contact and acknowledge their presence.

When guests are within five feet, greet them and offer assistance.

Always acknowledge a guest waiting to speak to you, even while you are on the phone.

One Stop Shopping

The "One Stop Shopping Rule" means to immediately address all of the guests' needs and requests. The guest will need to make only one contact (via telephone, approaching the bar, stopping you in a public area such as the pool deck, etc.) to receive anything (from a fax to a hamburger to an extra towel to summoning transportation). Remember, refer to the request, not to the guest. After the initial guest request, ask if there is anything else that you may get for the guest. Make certain that you communicate the request completely to the proper person. Guests should never have to make a second or follow-up call. It is our job to make certain that we fulfill all guests' requests and needs during the first contact and to ensure the prompt delivery of those items or services. Go the extra mile!

Again, we want to do everything we can to eliminate the word "No" from our vocabulary. We must be prepared to meet all guest requests to the best of our ability and we must be committed to meeting requests the first time they are made.

Section Ⅲ: Passage
Interpret the following passage into English.

顾客忠诚度

保持客户忠诚度显然是所有企业的主要目标。忠实的顾客意味着可靠的收入来源和持续的利润。因此,如何保持客户忠诚度便成为许多研究人员探讨的主题,这一点毫不奇怪。如果你是企业老板或经理,你应该了解有关顾客忠诚度的各种各样的理论,这是因为建立一个忠实的客户群是促进业务增长的关键。

客户满意度

要建立一个忠实的客户群,第一步就是要提高客户对你的产品和服务的满意度。专家通常建议,利用调查问卷对你的客人进行标准化的调查。提高客户满意度是一个连续的过程。问问客户他们希望哪方面得到改善,不断完善、继续询问都是该过程的一部分。最后,满意的顾客就变成了忠实的顾客。

期望确认

期望确认的过程是影响客户忠诚度的另一个关键因素。企业的忠实顾客都希望能得到他们期待的质量和服务。只要他们的期望能持续得到满足,他们就是忠诚的。企业一旦无法满足客户的期望,便失去了长期客户。因此,可靠性和一致性对保持顾客忠诚度来说是不可或缺的。

信任

信任,和期望确认一样,也是需要考虑的因素,不过,它更多的在于道德方面。如果客户认为企业的方针与自己的道德观念相一致,就会变得更加忠诚。这不仅涉及企业如何处理与客户之间的关系,也涉及企业如何处理与员工的关系。客户一旦觉得某个企业可以信任,也就是说,这个企业有可靠的道德价值观念,客户就有更充足的理由与之建立长期的关系。

发展

保持忠诚客户的一个关键挑战在于企业如何平衡保持忠诚客户与自身发展需求之间的关系。发展企业及建立客户群的策略与只关注于如何保持老客户的策略之间总需要一个权衡。企业发展到一定规模后,这种一致性很难保持。因此,如何协调二者之间的关系是一个重要的管理技能。

Section Ⅰ: Dialog

服务员:送餐服务。可以进去吗?

客人:Come on in.

服务员:夫人,您好。这是您要的午餐,牛排、鸡蛋、沙拉,还有咖啡。

客人:Thank you, sir. Just put them on the table, please.

服务员:好的。这是鲜花和蛋糕……

客人:What? I haven't ordered them, sir.

服务员:我知道。这是我们总经理送的。我们从您的登记卡上得知,今天是您丈夫的生日。

客人：Oh, it's very kind of you, sir. My friends told me this is a very special hotel. Now I know why. Please say thank you to your manager for us. My husband will be thrilled when he comes back. He'll be here in 5 minutes.

服务员：好的，夫人。

客人：Oh, here's a card. It says, "Happy birthday to you, Mr. Charles Jackson. You are indeed 75 years young. Many happy returns of the day." I couldn't thank you enough, sir. You know what?

服务员：什么？

客人：We plan to celebrate this evening.

服务员：所以，你们今天要庆祝两次啰？

客人：Exactly, sir.

服务员：嗯，既然今天对你们来说是个特殊的日子，我想我就不打扰了。

客人：What a thoughtful young man!

服务员：离开之前，夫人，请您在账单上签个字吧。

客人：OK.

服务员：在虚线上签。

客人：I will. Here it is.

服务员：谢谢。如果还需要别的，请给我们打电话。

客人：OK.

服务员：请慢用。再见。

客人：Bye.

Section Ⅱ：Passage

威斯汀餐饮服务条例（第二部分）

与客人交谈

每次与客人交谈，你都有机会为威斯汀创造一个积极的印象。与客人之间的积极互动，一方面有助于增加客人的满意度和忠诚度，另一方面也可以为我们提供重要的信息，以便于我们提高服务水平。

永远用一种积极的语调，表达真正的关切。

学会积极倾听。积极倾听是一种能力，它能让你把精力都集中到客人的要求或与客人的互动上去，能以适当的方式回应客人的要求。

与客人交谈时，要保持目光接触。

如果客人要求你重复或再解释一遍某个问题时，要保持耐心。

如果知道了客人的名字，就要经常称呼他的名字。

当你不知道客人的名字时，称呼"先生"或"夫人"。

每当提到酒店或餐饮部门时，永远不要说"他们"（they）、"他们"（them）、"他们的"（theirs），而要说"我们"（we）、"我们"（us）、"我们的"（ours）。

永远不要打探客人的隐私。

准确地回答所有问题。如果你不知道答案，不要说"我不知道"。相反，要告诉客人，你会找到答案的，并会马上告诉他。永远不要把客人推给别人。永远不要提供不准确的信息。要提前一步，掌握信息。

"十""五"准则

当客人在 10 英尺以内时，要微笑，要有眼神接触，承认他们的存在。

当客人在 5 英尺内时，和他们打招呼，并主动提供帮助。

永远不要冷落一个等着跟你说话的客人，即使你正在打电话也是一样。

一站式服务

"一站式服务原则"意味着立刻满足客人的所有需求。客人只需要打一个电话，去一下吧台，或者在公共区域（如泳池边）拦住你，就可以得到所需要的任何东西，如发一个传真、点一个汉堡、要一条毛巾或出租车预约等。记住，此处，需要关注的是客人的需求，而不是客人本身。客人提出请求以后，不妨问一下还有没有其他可以效劳的地方。务必把客人的请求传达给合适的人员，千万不能让客人打第二遍电话。我们的工作就是要确保和客人第一次接触时，就能满足其所有需求，及时提供所需物品或服务。要加倍努力啊。

重申一下，我们将想方设法从我们的服务语言中去掉"不"字；我们将竭力满足客人的所有需求；我们必须保证客人第一次提出请求时就能得到满足。

Section Ⅲ：Passage

Customer Loyalty

Maintaining customer loyalty is obviously a key goal for any business. Loyal customers mean a reliable revenue stream and a sustained profit. Not surprisingly, then, the subject of how you maintain customer loyalty has been one that many researchers have looked into. If you are a business owner or manager, there are a variety of theories on customer loyalty that you should be aware of, as building a base of loyal customers is key to the growth of a business.

Customer Satisfaction

The first step towards building a base of loyal customers is to improve the satisfaction that customers have with your products and services. Experts generally recommend performing a standardized survey of your customers using questionnaires. The process of improving customer satisfaction is continuous. Asking customers what they would like to see improve, making improvements and then asking again is all part of the process. In the end, satisfied customers are loyal customers.

Expectation Confirmation

The process of expectation confirmation is another key to customer loyalty. Customers who are loyal to a business develop a certain idea of quality and service that they expect to be confirmed. As long as their expectations continue to be confirmed, they are loyal. Businesses lose long-term customers when they cease to meet the expectations. As a result, reliability and consistency are necessary to maintain loyalty.

Trust

Trust is a consideration similar to expectation confirmation, but with more of an ethical dimension. Customers will be more loyal to businesses that they feel matching their own ethical concerns. This involves not only how a business deals with their customers, but their employees as well. By feeling that they can trust a business, in the sense that it has reliable ethical values, customers will have an additional reason to build a long-term relationship.

Growth

A key challenge in maintaining loyal customers is how a business balances this concern with its need for growth. There will always be some tradeoff between the strategies that are necessary to grow a business and build its customer base and those that focus solely on maintaining older customers. It can be hard to maintain consistency when a business has grown to a significant degree. Negotiating this balancing act is a key management skill.

第5单元
客房服务

Housekeeping Service

Text A

Section Ⅰ: Dialog
Interpret the following dialog alternatively into English and Chinese.

客房服务员: Housekeeping. May I come in?
客人: 请进。
客房服务员: I hope I'm not disturbing you.
客人: 一点也没有。
客房服务员: My name is Lisa. I'm a floor attendant. The Front Desk sent me up here. Is there anything I can do for you, sir?
客人: 我有几个朋友要过来。可是,你看,我刚冲了个澡,洗手间里乱糟糟的。请帮我收拾一下,好吗?
客房服务员: At your service, sir.
客人: 对了,丽莎,有衣服要洗,怎么办?
客房服务员: If you have any, please just leave it in the laundry bag behind the bathroom door. The laundry man comes over to pick it up every morning at 10 o'clock.
客人: 好的。这里有干洗服务吗?
客房服务员: Yes, sir. We offer free dry cleaning service. When you get your clothes back, you will find that they are as good as new.
客人: 太好了。我的确有一些衣服要洗。如果服务员今天来取,什么时候能送回来?
客房服务员: It depends, sir. If all goes well, you will have them back tomorrow. But, if many of our guests ask for laundry service, it might take a longer time. Anyway, you can have your laundry back the day after tomorrow at the latest.
客人: 好的。如果洗衣时造成损坏,怎么办?
客房服务员: Generally speaking, this won't happen. If, I mean if, it does happen, the hotel should certainly pay for it. However, the indemnity shall not exceed 10 times the laundry.
客人: 明白了。如果我想自己洗呢?
客房服务员: We do have a laundromat in the basement. In that case, you need to have some coins ready. Suppose you don't have any, the laundry man there will help you out.

客人：太感谢了。
客房服务员：Is there anything else I can do for you, sir?
客人：暂时没有。谢谢你提供的信息。
客房服务员：You are welcome, sir. Shall I do the bathroom now?
客人：请。

Section II: Passage
Interpret the following passage into Chinese.

Rules & Regulations of Hotel Rooms

Hotel rooms come in a variety of styles and price ranges, from cheap motels to luxury five star resorts and everything in between. Despite differences in decor and price, one thing most hotels have in common is a set of rules and regulations. The rules and regulations are put in place to keep hotel guests and employees safe and protect hotel property from damage. Failure to obey these rules can result in fees or fines to cover hotel room damages, removal from the hotel or possibly even arrest.

Smoking

Some hotels are completely non-smoking. The policy usually includes hotel-room balconies and patios. Some hotels designate smoking and non-smoking rooms. If you smoke in a non-smoking room, you will likely be fined hundreds of dollars and possibly asked to leave. If you are a smoker, reserve a smoking room if one is available at your hotel, or speak to the front desk about where you are allowed to smoke on the property.

Number of Guests

Most regular hotel rooms are designed for two adults. If you have more than two people staying in the room, the hotel will likely charge an additional fee for each extra guest, though some hotels let children stay free. Do not put more than four adults in the room unless the hotel's policy permits that many people. Too many people staying in one room might be a fire code violation, and you might be fined or removed from the hotel. Consider reserving more than one room to accommodate everyone, or reserve a larger suite if the hotel has one available.

Hotel Reservations Requirements

You must be 18 or older to rent a room at most hotels. If you lie about your age, you are violating hotel rules. Also, if you reserve a hotel room for a minor and do not stay there, you might be liable for any damage done. Unaccompanied minors may not reserve hotel rooms or stay in hotel rooms on their own.

Most hotels require a major credit card to reserve the room. You can pay cash at the end of your stay, but do not be surprised if there is a temporary charge on your card for a few days after your stay. Most hotels authorize a security deposit on your card to cover any possible damages to the room. Once the hotel verifies that the room is undamaged and that you did not violate any hotel policies, your security deposit will be refunded.

Pets

Hotels have clear pet policies: some allow pets, others do not. If you stay in a hotel that strictly does not allow pets, you will likely be fined if you bring your furry friend into the room. Hotels that do allow pets often require advance notice that you will be bringing a pet, and usually charge extra or make you pay a security deposit that is refunded after you check out and the staff verifies that no damage was done to the room. Exotic pets are rarely allowed in hotels; most pet-friendly hotels allow only common domestic pets like cats and dogs.

Section Ⅲ: Passage
Interpret the following passage into English.

客 房 部

酒店客房部可以视为酒店的使者，因为正是他们的奉献和责任使酒店的形象得以维护。客房部具体负责客房和店内其他区域，为客人提供一个干净舒适的环境。通过清洁和整理公共空间，客房部确保客人看到的、感受到的一切都能为酒店留下一个积极的印象。

功能

酒店客房部的主要作用是清洁客房。客房部与前台紧密合作，待房间清理干净、可以入住时，通知前台。尽管一提到客房部，人们首先想到房间清洁和消毒任务，但其实客房服务人员还负责其他领域，如公共洗手间、会议室和办公室等地方。客房部常常负责洗衣业务，包括洗涤床上用品及员工制服。在一些酒店，客房服务人员还负责迷你酒吧存货清查和送餐服务。

类型

客房部有很多职务。一般来说，有一名主管，有时称为行政主管，负责部门和员工的管理。客房部也设有总监，检查具体工作，管理一线员工，包括客房服务员、洗衣服务员、开夜床服务员和公共场所服务员。此外，还有其他员工，负责办公室的电话接听和员工的任务分派。在一些酒店，办公室人员还负责管理失物招领。

规模

客房部往往是酒店里最大的部门。员工的数量与酒店的规模有关，分正式员工和临时工两种。正式员工数量的确定常常基于一个客房服务员当班时能清洁的房间数量。客房部员工总数是基于每一个客房服务员每天能清洁的房间数量，但日程安排取决于客房入住率和／或其他特殊项目。

日程安排

酒店的客房部24小时运转，但大部分员工上白班。上白班的员工通常是客房服务员，从早上开始打扫房间。客房部的日程安排取决于客房入住率，所以，客房部最繁忙的时段是客人早上退房和下午入住时间。开夜床服务员晚上上班，这样，可以在晚上为客人提供开夜床服务。洗衣服务员和公共场所服务人员上班时间不固定。

工具

客房服务员通常使用客房服务车推着所需要的工具和客房必需品，这样，她们就可以把设备等东西送到每一个房间。车上装着化学制品和清洁用品，用于客房和浴室表面的清洁。车上也载有真空吸尘器、扫帚和垃圾袋。尽管地毯清洗机和臭氧消毒机并不是带到每一个房间，但是，如果房间需要额外的清洁维护，可以随时使用。

Section Ⅰ：Dialog

客房服务员：客房服务。可以进去吗？

客人： Yes, please.

客房服务员：但愿没有打扰您。

客人： Not a bit.

客房服务员：我叫丽莎，是楼层服务员。前台让我来的。有什么能为您效劳的吗，先生？

客人： Yes. I'm having some friends over. But, you see, I just took a shower and the bathroom is quite a mess now. Will you please tidy up a bit in it?

客房服务员：愿意为您效劳，先生。

客人：By the way, Lisa, what shall I do if I have any laundry?

客房服务员：如果有衣服要洗，请把它放在洗手间门后的洗衣袋里。服务员每天上午10点来取。

客人：Good. Do you have a dry cleaning service here?

客房服务员：有的，先生。干洗服务是免费的。等衣服回来，您就会发现，它们变得像新的一样，完好如初。

客人： That's great. I do have some clothes to be washed. If the laundry man comes to collect the laundry bag today, when can I have them back?

客房服务员：这要看情况，先生。如果一切正常，明天就可以取回来。可是，如果洗衣服的客人比较多，就需要更长一点时间了。不管怎么样，最迟后天可以取回来。

客人：Good. What if there is any laundry damage?

客房服务员：一般来说，这种事情不会发生。如果，我是说如果，发生了，酒店会赔偿的。不过，赔偿金不会超衣服原价的 10 倍。

客人：I see. What if I want to do the laundry myself?

客房服务员：我们的确有自助洗衣店，在地下室。那样的话，您得自备硬币。如果没有，那里的服务员会帮您解决的。

客人：That's very kind of you.

客房服务员：还有什么可以为您效劳的吗，先生？

客人：Not for the moment. Thank you for your information.

客房服务员：不客气，先生。我现在可以收拾洗手间了吗？

客人：Yes. Please do.

Section II: Passage

酒店房间规章制度

从廉价的汽车旅馆到豪华的五星级度假胜地以及其他介于两者之间的酒店，客房风格迥异，价格不同。尽管装潢和价格差异较大，但是，大多数酒店都有一个共同点，那就是都有"规章制度"。规章制度旨在保证客人和员工的安全，保护酒店财产免受破坏。未能遵守这些规则会被罚款、赔偿房间损失、驱逐出店，甚至锒铛入狱。

吸烟

一些酒店完全禁烟，通常包括客房阳台和天井。一些酒店分为吸烟房间和无烟房间。在无烟房间里吸烟，可能受到数百美元的罚款，甚至可能被勒令离店。如果你是一名吸烟者，就尽可能预订一个吸烟房间，或者问问前台，店里哪里可以吸烟。

客房人数

一般来说，一间客房住两名成年人。如果有其他人住在房间里，酒店将根据人头收取额外的费用，不过，有些酒店儿童免费。一间客房里不要超过四个成年人，酒店规定允许的例外。太多人住在一个房间，可能违反消防条例，你可能会被罚款或被勒令离店。尽量预订多个房间，满足每个人的需要，或者，可能的话，预订一个大的套房。

酒店预订要求

大部分酒店要求客人年满 18 岁或 18 岁以上。隐瞒年龄，将违反酒店规定。同样，如果你为未成年人预订一个房间却没有入住，出现任何损失你都要承担。无人陪伴的未成年人不得预订客房或自己住在里面。

大多数酒店需要一张主流信用卡才能预订房间。你当然可以在离店时用现金支付，但是，如果你入住几天后临时收费，请不要感到惊讶。大多数酒店要求支付押金，以便日后赔偿所有可能造成的损失。一旦酒店确认房间完好无损，而且你也没有违反酒店任何规定，你的押金将如数退还。

宠物

酒店有明确的宠物政策：有些允许带宠物，有些不行。如果你入住一家禁带宠物的酒店，却把毛茸茸的朋友带进房间，可能会遭到罚款。允许带宠物的酒店往往需要你预先通知，而且，通常会收取额外费用或让你交保证金，离店时待员工确认房间没有任何损坏后再退还给你。外来（异国）宠物一般不得带入酒店；大多数宠物友好型酒店只允许携带普通家养宠物，如猫、狗等。

Section Ⅲ: Passage

The Housekeeping Department

Hotel housekeeping departments can be considered hotel ambassadors because of their dedication and responsibility in maintaining the hotel's image. Housekeeping performs detailed work in guest rooms and hotel areas to provide a clean, comfortable environment for hotel guests to enjoy. Through cleaning and organizing public spaces, housekeeping departments ensure that what the guests see and experience result in a positive impression of the property.

Function

The primary role of the hotel's housekeeping department is cleaning guest rooms. Housekeeping works closely with front desk operations to communicate when rooms are clean and ready for guests to occupy. Although usually associated with cleaning and sanitizing guest rooms, housekeepers are also responsible for other areas, such as public restrooms, convention space and offices. Housekeeping departments often manage laundry operations, which includes washing linens as well as employee uniforms. At some hotels, housekeepers are responsible for mini-bar inventory and room service.

Types

Housekeeping departments include a variety of job titles. The department will generally have a director of housekeeping, sometimes called the executive housekeeper. This employee is responsible for managing the department and its employees. Housekeeping departments also have supervisors who inspect work and several types of line staff, including room attendants, laundry attendants, turn-down attendants and public space attendants. In addition, other housekeeping employees run the department office by answering phones and dispatching attendants. In some hotels, the office personnel are responsible for managing lost and found items.

Size

The housekeeping department is often the largest employee department in the hotel. The number of employees is relative to the size of the hotel, and may be a combination of full-time hotel employees and temporary leased labor. The number of full-time employees is generally based on the average number of rooms one housekeeper can clean in one shift. The housekeeping department's full size is based on the rooms per housekeeper per day formula, but daily scheduling depends on occupied rooms and/or special projects.

Schedule

Hotel housekeeping departments operate 24 hours each day, but the majority of employees work during the day. Day shift housekeepers are typically room attendants who begin cleaning rooms in the morning. The housekeeping schedule revolves around guest occupancy, so housekeeping departments are at their busiest between guest check-out in the morning and check-in in the afternoon. Turn-down attendants are scheduled for evening shifts, so they can perform nightly turn down in guest rooms. Laundry and public space attendants may work any shift.

Tools

Room attendants generally use a cart to hold their tools and supplies so they can bring the necessary equipment with them to each room. Carts are stocked with chemicals and cleaning supplies to clean surfaces in guest rooms and bathrooms. The cart also holds a vacuum cleaner, broom and trash bag. Although not brought to every room, carpet shampooers and ozone machines can be brought to rooms that require extra cleaning attention.

课文 2　　Text B

Section Ⅰ: Dialog

Interpret the following dialog alternatively into English and Chinese.

客人：Hello. Is that housekeeping service?
客房服务员：是的。有什么能为您效劳的吗，夫人？
客人： I'd like extra towels, please.
客房服务员：请问，您的房间号码是什么？

客人：2345.

客房服务员：2345号房间。好的，要加毛巾。没问题，夫人。我们马上给您送两条过去。

客人：And a toothbrush, and ... a razor for my husband, please.

客房服务员：一个牙刷，马上送过去。可是，对不起，我们不提供刮胡刀。您可以在一楼大厅的礼品店里买到的。

客人：I see. And ...

客房服务员：还有事吗？

客人：Something's wrong with the toilet.

客房服务员：怎么了？

客人：The toilet doesn't flush properly. The water closet seems to be clogged.

客房服务员：对不起，夫人。我们马上处理。

(2分钟后)

客房服务员：Housekeeping service. May I come in?

客人：请进。

客房服务员：I'm here to fix the toilet.

客人：谢谢。

客房服务员：Did you use it just now, ma'am?

客人：没有。我进来时，就是这样。

客房服务员：Let me check. Well ... It just doesn't work. That's weird.

客人：你觉得可以马上修好吗？

客房服务员：I don't know, ma'am.

客人：那样的话，我觉得该换个房间。我有客人要来。

客房服务员：I think so, too, ma'am. Sorry for the inconvenience caused.

客人：没关系，又不是你的错。我马上给前台打电话。

客房服务员：OK. If you still want this room, we'll call you when the toilet is fixed.

客人：谢谢你的好意。你真是太好了。

客房服务员：Good luck.

客人：也祝你好运。

Section Ⅱ：Passage
Interpret the following passage into Chinese.

Housekeeping Service and Consumer Loyalty

Consumer loyalty pertains to the repeat business generated by returning customers, and to the positive attitudes of these customers towards specific companies and their associated products or services. Consumer loyalty is achieved by providing consistently good products and services, high quality customer service and problem resolution strategies and the offer of rewards and discounts for loyalty.

Consumer loyalty essentially falls into the two categories of attitude and behavior. When combined in varying degrees, these two categories can result in four potential outcomes: loyalty; no loyalty, spurious loyalty and latent loyalty.

Loyalty

Loyal consumers are what every marketer hopes to achieve. They regularly and repeatedly purchase products or services from the same vendors. They recommend and refer the vendors to others and they are immune to the marketing strategies of competitors.

No Loyalty

These customers have weak behavioral and attitude habits pertaining to specific vendors. They may base their purchasing decisions on wide-ranging factors, including spur-of-the-moment purchasing, strategic product placement, convenience and on-the-spot discounts.

Spurious Loyalty

These customers may have seemingly positive attitudes toward a specific vendor and may sometimes purchase that vendor's products. However, they are just as likely to purchase similar products from competitors. They may seek the gratification of being seen to favor popular and fashionable items that are currently trendy, while at the same time they will be influenced by cost. These factors will influence from whom they purchase.

Latent Loyalty

These customers have a very positive attitude towards a specific vendor, yet they have a weak repeat purchase behavior. These customers are difficult for marketers to influence because there are factors out of the marketer's control that cause this latent loyalty, such as reduced disposable income or unemployment.

Bearing that in mind, you, as a room attendant, can do something to impress the guest during a housekeeping service so as to help build customer loyalty. As is known to all, it takes more than a clean room to impress a guest with housekeeping service. A clean room is expected. As a matter of fact, the cleanliness does not even register in their minds, unless the room is not clean. It is the unexpected little touches consistently present each day that impress a guest and make them want to come back for another stay.

1. Place high-end soaps, shampoo, conditioner and hand lotion on the bathroom vanity as high-end toiletries will impress guests.

2. Provide a spa-quality terrycloth robe for each guest on a satin hanger in the bath, as a luxury robe makes guests feel pampered.

3. Fold the end of the toilet paper in an interesting shape.

4. Coffee in a room is a convenience guests will appreciate. Supply a coffee maker with regular and flavored premium coffee and all the necessary accessories for making a cup in the room.

5. Place a quality pen and pad of paper next to the telephone for taking notes.

6. Finding treats in the room makes a guest feel special. Place a fancy paper doily on each pillow with an expensive, individually wrapped piece of chocolate on each doily.

7. Provide an elegant fruit basket with big, fresh local fruits for the guests to enjoy, as a fruit basket will appeal to health conscious guests.

8. Place a hand-written note from the housekeeper on the dresser telling the guests that the housekeeper would be happy to get them anything they need to make their stay more comfortable.

Section Ⅲ: Passage
Interpret the following passage into English.

客房服务技能

没有客房部,酒店几乎无法运转。客房服务人员大都在特定的区域工作,如在洗衣房熨烫衣服、洗毛巾床单、打扫房间或其他区域。酒店客房服务技能包括很多方面,如清空垃圾、擦窗户、整理床铺等。美国劳工统计局预测,到2016年,客房服务方面的工作将增加15.8%。大多数客房服务人员领取的是最低工资,不过,总监的薪水能略高一点。

清洗方法

酒店培训客房服务人员具体的清洗方法。大部分酒店要求床铺整理达到一个特定的标准,或使用指定的清洁产品清洗浴室。在洗衣部工作的服务人员,熨烫和折叠床单也要达到明确标准。

清洁工具

客房服务人员在打扫房间时,要使用指定的工具,包括吸尘器、抹布和拖把。客房服务人员必须确保客房服务车上有充足的供应,这样,就不会浪费时间去客房部领取。

房间布置

准备客房时，房间布置至关重要。客人进屋后，要有一种舒适的感觉。很多酒店会增添一些特别的细节，如豪华沐浴产品、房间设计或床上用品，使之有别于其他酒店。客房服务人员必须根据酒店要求，按一定规格进行安排布置。其他职责还包括以特殊造型折叠和悬挂毛巾、安排小酒吧、开夜床服务、在床头放上巧克力等。

工伤

客房工作是一个对体力要求很高的工作，可能会导致人身伤害。客房服务人员背部拉伤的风险很大，腿脚受伤的概率也在增加。许多连锁酒店要求客房服务人员使用护腰，降低因弯腰或提举物品引起背肌拉伤的风险。松紧合适的鞋子也是非常重要的，循环软管有助于缓解腿部压力。

洗衣技能

客房服务人员每天要清洗、熨烫数百件床单、毛巾和衣服。许多人还要为客人清洗个人物品，而且，不能把客人的衣服损坏。客房服务人员的职责包括洗涤、折叠、熨烫和干洗等。

沟通技能

客房服务人员经常与客人碰面。他们必须具备良好的沟通能力，能够预测客人的需求。他们必须协助客人，满足其额外的要求，如索要额外的毛巾或私人物品等。客房服务人员必须确保客房干净舒适。此外，还需要解决因房间达不到客人要求而引起的投诉。

Section Ⅰ：Dialog

客人：你好。是客房服务部吗？

客房服务员：Yes. Can I help you, ma'am?

客人： 请给我加两条毛巾。

客房服务员：Your room number, please?

客人：2345.

客房服务员：Room 2345. OK. Extra towels it is. No problem, ma'am. We'll send up 2 towels right away.

客人：还要一个牙刷，嗯……再给我丈夫来一个刮胡刀。

客房服务员：One toothbrush coming right up. But I'm sorry we don't supply razors. You can buy one at our gift shop on the lobby.

客人：知道了。嗯……

客房服务员：Yes?

客人：马桶出问题了。

客房服务员：What's the trouble?

客人：抽水马桶不放水了。好像堵了。

客房服务员：Sorry, ma'am. We'll get right on it.

（2分钟后）

客房服务员：客房服务。可以进去吗?

客人：Come in, please.

客房服务员：我来修马桶。

客人：Thank you.

客房服务员：夫人，您刚才用过了吗?

客人：No. That's the way it was when I checked in.

客房服务员：我检查一下。嗯……就是不好使了。奇怪。

客人：Do you think you can fix it very soon?

客房服务员：不知道，夫人。

客人：In that case, I think I should change to another room. Someone is on his way over.

客房服务员：我觉得也是。对不起，给您带来不便。

客人：It doesn't matter. That's not your fault. I'll call the Front Desk right away.

客房服务员：好的。如果您还想住这个房间，等马桶修好了，我会通知您的。

客人：Thanks for your kindness. That's very nice of you.

客房服务员：祝您好运。

客人：Good luck to you, too.

Section II: Passage

客房服务与顾客忠诚度

顾客忠诚度与回头客带来的回头生意有关，与客户对特定公司及其相关产品或服务的肯定态度有关。客户忠诚度源自以下几个方面：始终提供优质产品、良好的服务、高质量的客户服务与问题解决策略，以及为培养客户忠诚度提供的优惠和折扣政策。

顾客忠诚度基本上分为态度和行为两个类别。当二者结合到不同的程度时，会出现四种潜在的结果：忠诚、不忠诚、虚假忠诚和潜在忠诚。

忠诚

忠诚的顾客是每一个营销人员都希望实现的目标。他们长期、反复地从同一供应商那里购买产品或服务。他们把供应商推荐给其他顾客，不受竞争对手营销策略的左右。

不忠诚

这些客户对特定供应商所持的行为和态度习惯不固定。他们的购买决定基于许多因素，包括冲动式购物、战略性产品焦点、随近逐便以及现场折扣等。

虚假忠诚

这些客户，从表面上看，对特定供应商持肯定态度，有时也会购买他们的产品。然而，他们同样也会从竞争对手那里购买类似产品。他们希望在别人眼里成为追逐时尚的人，并因此得到满足。与此同时，他们还会受到价格的影响。这些因素都会影响他们的最终决定。

潜在忠诚

这些客户对特定供应商抱肯定态度，但是，他们重复购买的行为较弱。这些客户很难受到营销人员的影响，因为营销人员无法控制某些导致潜在忠诚的因素，如可支配收入减少或失业等。

请记住，作为一名客房服务员，在提供客房服务时，可以做一些能给客人留下深刻印象的事情，帮助酒店建立顾客忠诚度。众所周知，客房服务不仅仅是为客人提供一个干净的房间。提供干净的房间是情理之中的事情。事实上，清洁的房间不会在客人心目中留下什么印象，除非这个房间不干净。正是那些每天都会出现的令人意想不到的小细节才会给客人留下深刻的印象，让他们想下次再来。

1. 在浴室盥洗台上，放上高端香皂、洗发水、护发素和护手霜，因为高端化妆品会给客人留下深刻的印象。

2. 在浴缸的包布衣架上，为每一位客人提供一件温泉浴场常见的厚绒布长袍，这会让客人感觉受到细心照顾。

3. 把洗手间卫生纸的一头折叠成有趣的形状。

4. 房间里的咖啡是很受客人欢迎的。房间里放置一台咖啡机，再放些常见的口味不错的优质咖啡及必要的调味品，这样，客人就可以自己在房间里沏上一杯咖啡了。

5. 电话旁边放置一支品质出众的钢笔和一个便笺，便于做笔记。

6. 房间里要是能找到"甜头"，客人会感觉很特别。在每个枕头上放置一个花式纸制桌巾，每个桌巾里面都放上一块独立包装的、价格不菲的巧克力。

7. 提供一个优雅的水果篮，里面盛着当地的新鲜水果，供客人享用，因为果篮对注重健康的客人很有吸引力。

8. 把一条手写的留言放在梳妆台上，告诉客人，客房服务员很高兴为他们提供在下榻期间所需要的任何物品，确保他们在此期间生活愉快。

Section Ⅲ: Passage

Hotel Housekeeping Skills

Hotels would find it impossible to run without a housekeeping staff. Most housekeepers work in specific areas of housekeeping, including in the laundry room, ironing and laundering towels and sheets, and cleaning rooms or other hotel areas. Hotel housekeeping skills encompass a wide range of skills from emptying trash, cleaning windows and bed making. The Bureau of Labor Statistics predicts an increase of 15.8% in housekeeping jobs by 2016. Most housekeepers are paid minimum wage, while some supervisors earn a slightly higher salary.

Cleaning Methods

Hotels train housekeepers in specific cleaning methods. Most require beds to be made to a particular standard or bathrooms to be cleaned using specified cleaning products. Housekeepers that work in the laundry are required to iron and fold linen to precise specifications as well.

Cleaning Tools

Housekeepers are required to use certain tools while cleaning a guest room. Tools range from vacuum cleaners to dust rags and mops. Housekeepers must make sure they stock their cleaning carts with enough supplies so they do not waste time retrieving items from the housekeeping department.

Organization

Room setting is essential when preparing a room for hotel guests. The hotel guest must feel comfortable on entering a room, and many hotels add special touches, such as luxury bath products, room design or bedding, that set them apart from other hotels. Housekeepers must arrange these special touches to specifications required by the hotel. Other duties may include folding and hanging towels in an appealing design, arranging a wet bar or turning down the bed and adding chocolate.

Job Injury

Housekeeping is a physically demanding job that can result in job injuries. Housekeepers are at risk of back strain and increased leg and feet injuries. Many hotel chains require housekeepers to wear back braces, lowering the chance of back strain from lifting or bending. Proper shoes are crucial, and circulation hose help to relieve stress to the legs.

Laundry Skills

Housekeepers launder and iron hundreds of sheets, towel and wash cloths daily. Many also launder personal items for guests and cannot ruin guest clothing. Duties include washing, folding, ironing and dry cleaning.

Communication Skills

Housekeepers encounter hotel guests on a regular basis. They are required to be able to communicate well and anticipate guest needs. They must assist with requests for additional items such as extra towels or personal items. Housekeepers have to ensure a guest room is clean and comfortable. Moreover, housekeepers are required to resolve any complaints that a guest may have with a room that does not meet the guest standards.

第6单元
餐厅就餐

At a Restaurant

 **Text A**

Section Ⅰ: Dialog
Interpret the following dialog alternatively into English and Chinese.

客人：A table for two, please.
服务员：好的，先生。二位想坐在吸烟区、非吸烟区，还是有空位就成？
客人：We prefer non-smoking section.
服务员：二位想坐靠窗的位置，还是靠过道的位置？
客人：Window seats, if possible.
服务员：那边有张桌子。请跟我来。
客人：Yes.
服务员：这是你们的座位，先生。
客人：Thank you.
服务员：二位是已经想好了吃什么，还是看看菜单？
客人：Two menus, please.
服务员：请稍等，我马上就来。
客人：OK. Can you take our order now?
服务员：当然。
客人：Kung Pao chicken, fish-flavored shredded pork, Ma Po tofu, fish filets in hot chili oil and hot and sour soup.
服务员：二位想喝点什么吗？
客人：Two beers, please.
服务员：冰镇的，还是常温的？
客人：Cold, please.
服务员：好的。二位想不想尝一下今日特餐？
客人：What is it?
服务员：麻辣小龙虾。
客人：Oh, it's one of my favorites. Is it authentic?
服务员：当然了，先生。我们所有的厨师都来自四川，他们是本市最好的厨师。
客人：OK. I'll have the special.
服务员：明智的选择。相信二位会喜欢的。就这么多吗，先生？
客人：That's it for now.
服务员：好的。马上就上。

Section II : Passage
Interpret the following passage into Chinese.

How to Build Customer Loyalty at a Restaurant

Building customer loyalty requires consistency. Consistent food preparation, regular table-side visits from the chef during meal service and a personal greeting from the host staff for reservation guests instill a sense of belonging that translates into repeat visits. Although you should make certain concessions for a guest, such as substituting an item for one of equal value, never compromise standards for customer loyalty. Although it's instinctual for a restaurateur to try to please each guest comprehensively to ensure a return visit, fulfilling every special request every time is far less effective when building customer loyalty than consistent service and food.

First, prepare the food in a consistent manner. Guests often fall in favor with specific dishes. Making sure the chef sets guidelines for his cooks concerning consistent measuring of ingredients, and their placement and presentation ensures that the guest receives the same dish prepared in the same manner each visit.

Second, instruct the host staff to greet guests with the proper salutation and their surnames if possible. The host staff should act affably but not overly friendly. However, a simple, "Good evening, Mrs. So-and-so, allow me to show you to your table," puts the guest at ease and grants her a feeling of familiarity.

Third, set up a frequent-diner program if operating a casual-themed restaurant. In a casual-themed restaurant there is no shame in offering perks to repeat guests if it doesn't cut into food costs excessively. Refer to your break-even point to determine if offering a discounted meal to repeat customers is viable. In fine dining, however, offering free food is impractical from a food-cost perspective, and lessens the perceived value of the meal to the guest.

Fourth, instruct your chef to perform table-side greetings during meal service. Table-side greetings from the chef provide an opportunity to receive guest feedback in an informal manner and displays professional courtesy. Guests return to restaurants when they feel recognized by the chef.

Fifth, incorporate daily specials if your restaurant uses a static menu. Daily specials serve as an opportunity to display a chef's creativity and provide a diversion from a static menu, or a menu that doesn't change regularly, and sets your establishment apart from others in its class.

Section Ⅲ: Passage
Interpret the following passage into English.

中国菜（第一部分）

中国菜包括中国不同地区不同风格的菜肴以及世界各地华人的菜肴。中国菜的历史可以追溯到数千年以前，后来，在不同时期、不同地区，由于气候不同，当地人的喜好不同，又发生了不一样的变化。随着时间的推移，随着帝国的扩张，随着近代前叶与周边国家以及近代与欧洲和新大陆的贸易往来，来自其他饮食文化的技法和原料也融入了中国人的菜肴。

中国菜的风格和口味也因阶层、地区和种族的不同而不同。其结果，一是我们常说的中国菜的原料、菜品、烹饪方法及饮食风格在世界上堪称独一无二；二是中国人在保持传统饮食文化精神的前提下，可以享用各种各样的美食，并因此而感到自豪。

中国菜有许多不同的风格，但也许最为有名、最具影响力的要属粤菜、鲁菜、苏菜（又叫淮扬菜）和川菜了。这些菜系，风格各异，主要是因为资源、气候、地理、历史、烹饪技术和生活方式各有不同。一种菜系可能偏爱使用大量的大蒜和洋葱，而非大量的辣椒和香料，而另一种菜系可能偏重于海鲜，而非肉类和家禽。

苏菜偏爱炖、煮，川菜则偏爱烘烤。种类之多，不一而足。大闸蟹是上海地区最受追捧的地方美食，因为当地的湖泊里就盛产这种螃蟹。北京烤鸭和"点心"是海外非常著名且备受欢迎的菜品。

由于原料、配料和烹饪方法的不同，加上文化的差异，各地出现了不同风味、不同材质的美食。许多传统地方菜系依赖原始的保存方法，如风干、腌制、浸泡和发酵等。

中国菜有八大菜系，即徽菜、粤菜、闽菜、湘菜、苏菜、鲁菜、川菜和浙菜。

参考答案

Section Ⅰ: Dialog

客人：请安排一张两个人的桌子。

服务员：OK, sir. Would you like to sit in the smoking section, non-smoking section or whatever comes open first?

客人：非吸烟区。

服务员：And do you want window seats or aisle seats?

客人：如果可能，还是靠窗户的座位。

服务员：We have a table over there. Would you follow me?

客人：好的。

服务员：Here you are, sir.

客人：谢谢。

服务员：Do you know what you want or would you like to see a menu?

客人：请拿两份菜单。

服务员：Just a second. I'll be right back.

客人：好了。你现在可以帮我们点菜吗？

服务员：I sure can.

客人：宫保鸡丁、鱼香肉丝、麻婆豆腐、水煮鱼片，外加一份酸辣汤。

服务员：Would you like anything to drink?

客人：两个啤酒。

服务员：Cold or at room temperature?

客人：冰镇的。

服务员：Good. Would you like to try our special today?

客人：什么特餐?

服务员：Hot and spicy crayfish.

客人：噢，那可是我最喜欢吃的东西之一。正宗吗？

服务员：You bet, sir. All our cooks are from Sichuan Province. They are the best in town.

客人：好的。那就来一个今日特餐。

服务员：Good choice. I'm sure you'll like it. Is that all, sir?

客人：先点这么多吧。

服务员：OK. They will be here in no time.

Section II: Passage

如何建立餐饮业顾客忠诚度

建立客人忠诚度需要前后一致。前后一致的厨艺，厨师长在客人就餐期间常到餐桌旁打招呼，餐厅人员对预约的客人进行私人问候，这一切都会让客人有一种归属感，并最终成为回头客。尽管你应该为客人做出某些让步，如替换等价物品，但是，在顾客忠诚度标准这个问题上，永远不能妥协。尽管从本能上来说餐厅老板都会千方百计去讨好每一位客人，期望其成为回头客，但是，就建立客人忠诚度而言，每次都答应客人特殊要求的功效远远低于每次都提供前后一致的服务和食物。

第一，以前后一致的方式准备食物。客人经常会喜欢上某些菜品。确保厨师长要为厨师制定烹饪指南，内容涉及菜品成分前后一致的标准，如何摆盘，如何上菜等，从而确保客人每次造访所点的菜品与以往完全一样。

第二，要求餐厅工作人员用恰当的方式迎接客人，如果可能，尽量用姓氏称呼客人。工作人员应该热情周到，但切忌巴结讨好。不过，一句简单的话语，如"某某太太，晚上好，请允许我送您去您的餐桌"，会让客人精神放松，让她产生一种亲切感。

第三，如果是一家休闲餐厅，最好制订一个"常客回馈计划"。在休闲餐厅，不必为给常客提供特殊待遇而感到尴尬，前提是不过度增加食品的成本。要根据收支平衡点来确定为回头客提供折扣餐是否可行。不过，在高档餐馆，从食品成本的角度来看，为客人提供免费食物不仅是不切实际的，而且也降低了食物在客人眼里的价值。

第四，要求厨师长在客人用餐期间到桌子旁和客人打招呼。这样既可以使其有机会以非正式的方式得到客人的反馈意见，又可以展示其职业厨师的风貌。客人认为自己让大厨认出来了，会再次光顾餐厅的。

第五，如果餐厅用的是固定菜单，最好增加每日特餐。每日特餐既可以使厨师长有机会展示自己的创意作品，又可以让客人暂时忘记固定菜单或不常更新的菜单，使你的餐厅有别于其他同类餐厅。

Section Ⅲ: Passage

Chinese Cuisine (Part One)

Chinese cuisine includes styles originating from the diverse regions of China as well as from Chinese people in other parts of the world. The history of Chinese cuisine dates back to thousands of years ago and has changed from period to period and in each region according to climate and local preferences. Over time, techniques and ingredients from the cuisines of other cultures were integrated into the cuisine of the Chinese people due both to imperial expansion and from the trade with nearby regions in pre-modern times and from Europe and the New World in the modern period.

Styles and tastes also vary by class, region, and ethnic background. This leads to an unparalleled range of ingredients, dishes, techniques, and eating styles in what can be called Chinese food, resulting in the Chinese priding themselves on eating a wide variety of foods while remaining true to the spirit and traditions of Chinese food culture.

A number of different styles contribute to Chinese cuisine but perhaps the best known and most influential are Cantonese cuisine, Shandong cuisine, Jiangsu cuisine (also known as Huaiyang cuisine) and Sichuan cuisine. These styles are distinctive from one another due to factors such as availability of resources, climate, geography, history, cooking techniques and lifestyle. One style may favor the use of lots of garlic and shallots over lots of chili and spices, while another may favor preparing seafood over other meats and fowl.

Jiangsu cuisine favors cooking techniques such as braising and stewing, while Sichuan cuisine employs baking, just to name a few. Hairy crab is a highly sought after local delicacy in Shanghai, as it can be found in lakes within the region. Peking duck and dim-sum are other popular dishes well known outside of China.

Based on the raw materials and ingredients used, the method of preparation and cultural differences, a variety of foods with different flavors and textures are prepared in different regions of the country. Many traditional regional cuisines rely on basic methods of preservation such as drying, salting, pickling and fermentation.

The Eight Culinary Traditions of China are Anhui, Cantonese, Fujian, Hunan, Jiangsu, Shandong, Sichuan, and Zhejiang cuisines.

 Text B

Section I: Dialog
Interpret the following dialog alternatively into English and Chinese.

客人: What a nice place!

服务员: 现在可以点餐了吗, 先生?

客人: Sorry, we haven't decided yet. Could you please give us a few more minutes?

服务员: 请慢慢点。

客人: Well, to start with, I'd like to have the minestrone for me and French onion soup for my wife.

服务员: 好的, 先生。嗯, 然后……

客人: Then, a sirloin steak, for medium rare, deep fried shrimp balls and a vegetable salad for my wife, and smoked salmon with caviar, fried rice with scallop, and Thai beef salad for me.

服务员: 需要喝点什么吗, 先生?

客人: Yes. A cup of coffee for my wife and a glass of red wine for me. By the way, what kind of coffee do you have?

服务员: 名牌咖啡我们都有, 先生。雀巢、UCC、皇室哥本哈根、克莱士、葛兰特、狄得利、薇吉伍德、皇家咖啡、达乐麦耶和上岛咖啡等。

客人：Make it UBC.

服务员：好的，上岛咖啡。

客人：What kind of red wine do you have available?

服务员：我们有法国的赤霞珠、梅鹿辄和黑皮诺，美国的宝石解百纳，意大利的桑娇维塞和西班牙的歌海娜。

客人：Cabernet Sauvignon.

服务员：好的，赤霞珠。要甜点吗，先生？

客人：Ice cream.

服务员：什么口味的，先生？

客人：Make it strawberry for my wife and vanilla for me.

服务员：好的，先生。

客人：Well, when we are finished, do I pay you or the cashier?

服务员：等您吃好了，我就把账单给您拿过来。

客人：Then…

服务员：您检查完了以后，要到那边的收银台结账。

客人：I see. Thank you very much.

服务员：不客气，先生。还需要什么，尽管叫我。非常愿意为您效劳。

客人：OK.

服务员：您的汤马上就到。希望您用餐愉快。

客人：Thank you. What did I say? This is my kind of place.

Section Ⅱ: Passage
Interpret the following passage into Chinese.

How to Create Customer Loyalty on the Web

Customer loyalty does not happen overnight with a web business or with an offline business. Customers are loyal to a hotel because the hotel understands the clients' needs and works to meet them. On the Internet, this customer care comes in the form of a well-designed website, live help and prompt answers to customer emails. Online incentives that offer new perks or discounts will also keep customers coming back to your site. Create customer loyalty by improving your virtual appearance and making your customers feel important.

First, design your hotel website. Place site navigational menus in easy-to-find places like the top and bottom of the page as well as on the sides.

Second, mark the "local" page link well and place it on the home page. This will direct the customer to your hotel in just one click, instead of them having to hunt for it.

Third, the reservation button feature should be easy to use and should work properly. Test this feature on a regular basis to insure that it remains user friendly.

Fourth, add links that answers the customers' basic questions. This area is often entitled the FAQ page. Providing timely answers to simple service questions can help to build customers' trust and loyalty in the website and your hotel as a natural result.

Fifth, set up regular hours to offer "Live Chat" or "Live Help" on your hotel page. This lets customers know that your hotel has someone available to answer their questions personally at specific times.

Sixth, encourage guests to your website to fill out a registration form to receive special deals and discounts you offer via email.

Seventh, send an electronic "Thank you!" via email to customers after every reservation.

Eighth, send a follow-up email within two weeks asking for feedback concerning the customer's hotel services, and online booking experience. Thank them for their feedback.

Ninth, deal with customer complaints according to your policy, apologize personally for poor services or inconveniences caused, and try to compensate for their losses, and if possible, offer a special price for them next time they come. That way you will probably keep your customers instead of losing them.

Section Ⅲ: Passage
Interpret the following passage into English.

中国菜（第二部分）

徽菜

徽菜是源自中国黄山地区的烹饪风格，与苏菜类似，不过，海鲜菜品不多，更偏重于当地各种各样的草本植物和蔬菜。安徽省在新鲜竹子和蘑菇作物方面有得天独厚的资源。

粤菜

一般来说，粤菜很清淡。"点心"是一个粤语词，指的是各种丰盛的"小吃"。这些一口大小的食物是利用传统烹饪方法制成的，如煎、蒸、炖、烤等，其目的是让人可以同时品尝多种美食，其中包括饭团、糯米鸡、萝卜酥、面包甜点、云吞、炒青菜、粥品、各种汤等。广东风格的就餐方式，即"饮茶"，指一边品尝各种各样的"点心",一边喝茶。"饮茶"就是"喝茶"的意思。

闽菜

闽菜受福建沿海位置和多山地区的影响。林地的美味特产,如食用蘑菇和竹笋等,也得到利用。刀功在闽菜中非常重要,刀功可以改善海鲜及其他食品的口感、香味和质地。闽菜通常汤水较多,烹饪方法包括炖、焖、蒸、煮等。

湘菜

湘菜的最大特点是香辣,颜色较重。常见的烹饪方法包括焖、煎、煲、炖、烟熏等。由于该地区农业产量高,因而取材广泛。

苏菜

苏菜是中国菜的一个主要组成部分,其自身又由扬州菜、南京菜、苏州菜和镇江菜组成,以其别具一格的风格和品味闻名于世,在长江下游尤受欢迎。

鲁菜

鲁菜有着悠久的历史,一度成为御膳房的重要组成部分,在中国北方广为流行。鲁菜囊括了各种各样的烹饪方法和海鲜原料。

川菜

川菜源自中国西南部的四川省,味道醇浓。川菜之刺激、之辛辣源于大蒜、辣椒以及四川花椒和朝天椒的大量使用。花生、芝麻酱和姜也是川菜的主要配料。

浙菜

浙菜源自浙江当地的烹饪风格。菜品不油不腻,味道鲜美,滋味醇和,香味醇厚。浙菜至少有四种不同的风格,每一种风格都来自不同的城市。杭州菜菜品丰富,多用竹笋;绍兴菜专攻家禽和淡水鱼的烹饪;宁波菜的特长是海鲜;上海菜则是浙菜各大风格的集大成,点心也很有名。

Section Ⅰ: Dialog

客人:这地方真不错!
服务员:Are you ready to order now, sir?
客人:不好意思,还没想好呢。再给我们一点时间,好吗?
服务员:Take your time, please.
客人:嗯,先给我来个蔬菜面条汤,给我夫人来个法式洋葱汤。
服务员:OK, sir. And then...
客人:然后,给我夫人来一盘沙朗牛排,要三分熟、一份泰式虾球、一份蔬菜沙拉;给我来一份烟熏鲑鱼配鱼子酱、一份金银蛋瑶柱炒饭和一份泰式牛肉沙拉。

服务员：Would you like anything to drink, sir?

客人：是的。给我夫人一杯咖啡，给我一杯红葡萄酒。对了，你们这里都有什么咖啡？

服务员：We have all the big names here, sir. They are Nescafe, UCC, Royal Copenhagen, Kreis Kaffee, Grandos Coffee, Tetley, Wedgwood, Royal Flavor, Dallmayr, and UBC Coffee.

客人：上岛吧。

服务员：OK. UBC it is.

客人：都有什么红葡萄酒？

服务员：We have Cabernet Sauvignon, Merlot and Pinot Noir from France, Ruby Cabernet from America, Sangiovese from Italy and Grenache from Spain.

客人：赤霞珠。

服务员：OK. Cabernet Sauvignon. Anything for dessert, sir?

客人：冰激凌。

服务员：What flavor would you like, sir?

客人：我夫人要草莓味的，我要香草味的。

服务员：OK, sir.

客人：嗯，吃完饭后，我是跟你结账，还是去收银台结账？

服务员：When you are done, I'll bring your bill.

客人：然后……

服务员：After you check your bill, you are expected to pay the cashier over there.

客人：明白了。多谢。

服务员：You are very welcome, sir. If you need anything else, just call me. I'm only too glad to serve you.

客人：好的。

服务员：Your soups will be here in a minute. I hope you will enjoy your meal.

客人：谢谢。我说什么来着？这才是我喜欢的地方。

Section II：Passage

如何通过网络建立顾客忠诚度

顾客对线上企业或线下企业的忠诚度不会在一夜之间建立起来。顾客之所以会忠于某个酒店，是因为该酒店了解顾客的需要，并努力予以满足。在互联网时代，顾客服务的形式包括精心设计的网站、即时帮助以及对客人邮件的即时回复。在线奖励，如新的优惠政策或折扣，也会让顾客重新回到你的网站来。你可以通过改善在线形象，让顾客觉得受到重视，来创建顾客忠诚度。

第一，设计酒店网站。网站的导航菜单要放在醒目的地方，如网页的顶部、底部，也可以放在两边。

第二，把"本地"页面链接标记好，放到主页上去。这样，一键就可以把顾客带到你的酒店，而无须顾客自己去寻找。

第三，"预订按钮"功能应易于使用，且能正常使用。定期测试这一功能，确保它能正常工作。

第四，添加"回答顾客基本问题"的链接。这就是通常所说的"常见问答"页面。及时回答顾客提出的简单服务问题，有助于客人对你的网站产生信任，并最终对你的酒店建立忠诚度。

第五，在酒店页面上定时进行"即时聊天"或提供"即时帮助"。这让顾客明白，你的酒店有专人在特定时间里亲自为他们解答疑问。

第六，鼓励顾客在酒店网站上注册，这样，可以通过电子邮件收到酒店提供的特别优惠和折扣信息。

第七，每次预订后，都要通过电子邮件向顾客道一声"谢谢"。

第八，顾客离店两周后，再发一封电子邮件，了解一下顾客对酒店服务的看法以及在线预订的体验。感谢他们提出反馈意见。

第九，根据酒店政策处理客人投诉，为劣质服务或带来的不便亲自道歉，设法弥补客人的损失。另外，如果可能的话，顾客再来时给他一个优惠的价格。这样，你可能会留住顾客，而不是失去他们。

Section Ⅲ: Passage

Chinese Cuisine (Part Two)

Anhui Cuisine

Anhui cuisine is derived from the native cooking styles of the Huangshan Mountains region in China and is similar to Jiangsu cuisine, but with less emphasis on seafood and more on a wide variety of local herbs and vegetables. Anhui Province is particularly endowed with fresh bamboo and mushroom crops.

Cantonese Cuisine

Generally speaking, Cantonese cuisine is very light. Dim sum is a Cantonese term for small hearty dishes. These bite-sized portions are prepared using traditional cooking methods such as frying, steaming, stewing and baking. It is designed so that one person may taste a variety of different dishes. Some of these may include rice rolls, lotus leaf rice, turnip cakes, buns, *shui jiao*-style dumplings, stir-fried green vegetables, congee porridge, soups, etc. The Cantonese style of dining, *yum cha*, combines the variety of dim sum dishes with the drinking of tea. *Yum cha* literally means "drink tea".

Fujian Cuisine

Fujian cuisine is influenced by Fujian's coastal position and mountainous terrain. Woodland delicacies such as edible mushrooms and bamboo shoots are also utilized. Slicing techniques are valued in the cuisine and utilized to enhance the flavor, aroma and texture of seafood and other foods. Fujian cuisine is often served in a broth or soup, with cooking techniques including braising, stewing, steaming and boiling.

Hunan Cuisine

Hunan cuisine is well known for its hot spicy flavor, fresh aroma and deep color. Common cooking techniques include stewing, frying, pot-roasting, braising, and smoking. Owing to the high agricultural output of the region, there are many varied ingredients for Hunan dishes.

Jiangsu Cuisine

Jiangsu cuisine is one of the major components of Chinese cuisine, which consists of the styles of Yangzhou, Nanjing, Suzhou and Zhenjiang dishes. It is very famous all over the world for its distinctive style and taste. It is especially popular in the lower reaches of the Yangtze River.

Shandong Cuisine

Shandong cuisine has a long history. It once formed an important part of the imperial cuisine and was widely promoted in North China. Shandong cuisine features a variety of cooking techniques and seafood ingredients.

Sichuan Cuisine

Sichuan cuisine, which originated from the Sichuan Province of southwestern China, is famed for its bold flavors, particularly the pungency and spiciness resulting from the liberal use of garlic and chili peppers, as well as the unique flavor of the Sichuan peppercorn and pod pepper. Peanuts, sesame paste and ginger are also prominent ingredients in this style.

Zhejiang Cuisine

Zhejiang cuisine derives from the native cooking styles of the Zhejiang region. The dishes are not greasy, having instead a fresh, soft flavor with a mellow fragrance. The cuisine consists of at least four styles, each of which originated from different cities in the province. Hangzhou style is characterized by rich variations and the use of bamboo shoots. Shaoxing style specializes in poultry and freshwater fish, and Ningbo style, in seafood. Shanghai style, a combination of different Zhejiang styles, is also very famous for its dim sum.

第7单元
兑换外币

Foreign Currency Exchange

Text A

Section Ⅰ: Dialog
Interpret the following dialog alternatively into English and Chinese.

服务员: Good evening, sir. Can I help you?
客人: 酒店里可以兑换货币吗?
服务员: Sure.
客人: 请问,具体怎么办呢?
服务员: First of all, you need to fill out an exchange form.
客人: 哪儿有?
服务员: Right here on this counter, sir. Here it is.
客人: 可是,这是汉语的。不好意思,我看不懂。
服务员: Don't worry, sir. Let me help you. Give me your passport, please.
客人: 给。
服务员: And you are Tim Romney?
顾客: 是的。
服务员: Good. Why not take a chair while I'm filling out the exchange memo for you?
客人: 谢谢。
服务员: OK, Mr. Romney, now tell me what kind of foreign currency you have and what kind of currency you'd like to change into.
客人: 我有一些美元,还有一些欧元,想兑换成人民币。
服务员: US dollars and Euros. OK, how much do you want to change?
客人: 400美元,500欧元。对了,今天的汇率是多少?
服务员: 689.35 yuan for 100 dollars, and 731.68 yuan for 100 Euros.
客人: 今天的汇率比昨天的略高一点。
服务员: Yes. You know, the exchange rates fluctuate every day.
客人: 我知道。现在可以为我兑换了吗?
服务员: I'm sorry, Mr. Romney, I'm afraid we don't have that much cash on hand.
客人: 你的意思是……
服务员: Yes. If you agree, I'll change the 400 US dollars for you today, and you come back tomorrow to change the 500 Euros. What do you say?
客人: 我还能说什么呢? 我想只能那样了。好吧。

服务员：Sorry, Mr. Romney. How would you like your money?

客人：什么样的都成。

服务员：OK. ... Here's your money, 2757.64 yuan in total. Check it, please.

客人：没错。

服务员：And here are your passport and your receipt.

客人：多谢。我明天同一时间过来。

服务员：Anytime. See you then.

Section Ⅱ：Passage

Interpret the following passage into Chinese.

Advantages of Using Credit Cards

Credit cards are one of life's most useful financial management tools. Used properly, a credit card can have many advantages. Such advantages include the potential to earn financial rewards, the ability to avoid carrying large amounts of cash and the opportunity to build up a sound credit history.

What are credit cards?

Credit cards are plastic cards that allow users to get a cash advance or buy items on credit. Credit is borrowed money that must be paid back within a certain time frame. Credit users are typically charged interest on the borrowed money if the money is not paid back in full within that time.

Potential to Earn Rewards

Many credit cards offer users the opportunity to earn various kinds of rewards if the card is used. These rewards can range from airline tickets to discounts on books and clothing. Some cards even directly reward users with cash.

Incentives are generally earned based on how much money is charged on the credit card. Incentives can be dispensed on a monthly or yearly basis. Rewards can often be used directly or carried over from year to year.

Building up a Credit History

Another advantage of using credit cards is the chance to build up a credit history. A credit history is a demonstration that the user is able to pay back money he borrows in a timely manner. A credit history can be created by buying low-cost items for a few months and then paying for them promptly.

A good credit history is important in several ways. Certain jobs require a credit check as part of the application process. A high credit score can be a way of demonstrating that the applicant is trustworthy. A good credit history is also useful when purchasing costly items such as a house. Applicants with good credit histories generally qualify for lower mortgage rates. A lower mortgage rate means a less costly monthly housing payment.

No Cash Required

Credit cards also allow the user to substitute the card for cash to use as payment for items. This is useful because carrying cash can have disadvantages. A $20 bill can easily be lost. A wallet can get stolen. If you lose cash you are out that amount of money forever. Using a credit card means you cannot lose your money. If your credit card is stolen and used, as long as you contact the credit card company within a reasonable time frame you cannot be held liable if the card is used without your permission.

Traveling Abroad

Credit cards can also come in handy if you're traveling abroad. Many places overseas accept commonly used credit cards. Using a credit card means that you don't have to be troubled with local currencies. A credit card may also offer users better exchange rates than can be found in local banks or stores.

Good Records

Every time you buy an item with a credit card, you will get a bill. At the end of the year many credit card companies will send users an itemized record of their exact purchases. This record can allow users to look closely at their buying habits. If you are trying to reduce your expenses you can find out exactly where your money goes each month.

A credit card record also serves as an additional receipt for purchases. If you get into a dispute with a merchant the credit card record can be used as additional evidence to bolster your claims.

Section Ⅲ: Passage
Interpret the following passage into English.

在中国如何兑换货币

在中国，兑换货币是一件非常简单的事情。中国的货币是元，又称人民币。"人民币"的意思就是"人民的货币"。在中国，每天都会形成新的人民币汇率，而且，所有货币兑换处都要公示。人民币汇率每天都会上下波动。所以，不要因此感到惊讶。

一、出发前，直接去设在国际机场的银行兑换。这也许能使游客快速离开中国机场，但是，汇率可能没有在中国高。

二、到达后，兑换成人民币。在中国主要的国际机场，具有货币兑换资格的有四大银行，它们是中国银行、中国工商银行、中国农业银行和中国建设银行。这些国有银行在北京、上海、广州和香港等地的国际机场都有分支机构。

三、在中国兑换货币时，需要带护照。正式的货币兑换单要求出纳员检查游客的护照，并登记身份证号码。一些银行会复印你的护照。填好货币兑换单，把单据、护照和现金一起放在出纳窗口，耐心等待。

四、如果需要兑换一大笔钱，等到了酒店以后再说。大多数三星级或三星级以上的酒店都有货币兑换柜台。机场出租车司机希望你用当地的钱支付车费。然而，货币兑换柜台可能不是全天营业，所以，到了以后先问一问。

五、去银行兑换。中国到处都有银行，每周营业 7 天，重大节日除外。有些是非常小的分支机构，提供有限的服务，有的则是雄伟壮观的大厦。许多银行都有一个排队取号系统，并把数字显示在出纳员的窗口上。不同的窗口，功能不同，但有人会把顾客引领到正确的窗口。

六、温馨提示。重要的文件要保存好。挂在脖子上的钱包很值得购买，至少在穿过拥挤的机场时如此。

中国农业银行提供西联汇款服务，星期天除外。

不要在当地银行兑换大量的现金，除非银行就在酒店附近。问酒店索要一个保险箱，把货币和贵重物品都保存在里面。

Section Ⅰ : Dialog

服务员：先生，晚上好。有什么能为您效劳的吗？
客人：Yes. Can I change money in this hotel?
服务员：可以。
客人：Can you tell me how to go about it?
服务员：首先，您要填一张兑换单。
客人：Where can I get it?
服务员：就在这个柜台上，先生。给您。
客人：But it's written in Chinese. Sorry I can't read it.
服务员：放心吧，先生。我来帮您。请把您的护照给我。
客人：Here you are.
服务员：您叫提姆·罗姆尼？
客人：Yes.

服务员：好的。请坐，我来给您填兑换单。

客人：That's very kind of you.

服务员：好的，罗姆尼先生，现在请告诉我，您有什么样的外币，想兑换成什么币种。

客人：I have some US dollars and some Euros, and I want to change them into RMB.

服务员：美元和欧元。好的，您想兑换多少？

客人：400 US dollars and 500 Euros. By the way, what are the rates today?

服务员：100美元兑换689.35元人民币，100欧元兑换731.68元人民币。

客人：Today's rates are a bit higher than those of yesterday.

服务员：是的。您知道，汇率每天都在浮动。

客人：I know. Can you change them for me now?

服务员：不好意思，罗姆尼先生，我们恐怕没有那么多现金。

客人：You mean...

服务员：没错。如果您同意的话，今天为您兑换400美元，明天来给您兑换那500欧元。您看怎么样？

客人：What else can I say? I guess that's that. Fine.

服务员：不好意思，罗姆尼先生。您要什么面值的？

客人：Any kind will do.

服务员：好的。……这是您的钱。一共2757.4元。您点一下。

客人：That's right.

服务员：这是您的护照和收据。

客人：Thanks a lot. I'll come back at the same time tomorrow.

服务员：不客气。到时候见。

Section Ⅱ ：Passage

使用信用卡的好处

信用卡是生活中最有用的理财工具之一。如果使用得当，信用卡具备很多优点，包括可能获得经济上的回报、避免随身携带大量现金、有机会建立良好的信用记录等。

信用卡是什么？

信用卡是允许用户进行现金透支或赊购商品的"塑料卡"。信贷即货币借贷，借款者必须在特定时间内偿还贷款。信贷用户如果不能在约定时间内全额偿还，必须支付利息。

可能获得奖励

许多信用卡为用户提供刷卡后获得各种奖励的机会。奖励范围从机票到图书和衣服的打折，应有尽有。有些信用卡甚至直接奖励用户现金。

奖金的多少通常取决于信用卡的消费金额。奖金可以是按月发放，也可以是按年发放。奖励通常可以直接使用或跨年使用。

建立信用记录

使用信用卡的另一个优点，是有机会建立个人信用记录。信用记录表明用户有能力及时偿还借款。通过在几个月内购买低价商品然后立即支付，可以创建个人信用记录。

良好的信用记录在若干方面都很重要。某些工作要求对申请人进行信用核查，这是员工录用程序中一个不可或缺的部分。信用等级高，证明申请人值得信赖。良好的信用记录在购买昂贵的物品（如房屋）时，也十分有用。信用记录良好的申请人可以获得较低的抵押贷款利率，而较低的抵押贷款利率则意味着月供的费用更少。

无须携带现金

信用卡也允许用户用信用卡代替现金进行支付。这是非常有用的，因为携带现金有不少缺点。一张20美元的钞票很容易丢失，钱包也很容易被盗。如果你丢失了现金，就永远丢失了。使用信用卡意味着你的钱会完好无损。如果信用卡被盗用，只要你在合理的时间内联系信用卡公司，即使有人未经许可使用了你的信用卡，你也无须承担责任。

出国旅行

出国旅行，信用卡也能派上用场。海外许多地方都可以使用常用的信用卡。使用信用卡意味着你不必为兑换当地货币而烦恼。使用信用卡，其汇率也比当地银行或商店的汇率要高。

良好的记录

每次使用信用卡消费时，都会得到一个账单。到了年底，许多信用卡公司都会给用户寄去其所购买商品的详细清单。该清单可以让用户仔细反省自己的购买习惯。如果你想减少开支的话，你可以准确地找出每个月钱到底都花到哪里去了。

信用卡记录也可以作为用户购买商品的另一个收据。如果你与卖家发生争执，信用记录可以作为额外的证据来维护你的权益。

Section Ⅲ：Passage

How to Exchange Currency in China

Exchanging currency in China is a very straightforward transaction. The Yuan, or Renminbi, is the currency for China. Renminbi translates as "The People's Currency". Exchange rates for Renminbi are established each day in China and should be displayed wherever currency is exchanged. The rate fluctuates from day to day. So do not be surprised.

1. Go directly to the bank at the international airport before departure. This may allow visitors to leave the airport in China more quickly, but the exchange rates may not be as favorable as it would be in China.

2. Convert to Renminbi after arriving. The four banks with currency exchanges at major international airports in China are Bank of China, the Industrial and Commercial Bank of China, the Agricultural Bank of China, and the Construction Bank of China. These national banks all have branches in the major international airports in Beijing, Shanghai, Guangzhou and Hong Kong etc.

3. Have your passport in hand when converting currency in China. The official currency exchange form in China requires the teller to see visitor's passports and record the identification number. Some banks may make a photo copy of the passport as well. Fill out the currency exchange sheet, place it, the passport and cash in the teller window and wait.

4. Wait until arriving at the hotel to convert large sums. Most three star or better hotels have a currency exchange counter. The taxi driver from the airport will expect payment, and the counter may not be open all day, so ask upon arrival.

5. Go to a bank. There are banks all over China, which are open seven days a week, except for major holidays. Some are very small branch offices with limited services and others are impressive edifices. Many banks have a system for taking a number, and display the numbers above the teller windows. There are different windows for different functions, but visitors will be directed to the correct window.

6. Tips and warnings. Keep important documents safe. A neck wallet is a good investment, at least for making it through the crowded airport.

The Agricultural Bank of China offers Western Union services, except on Sundays.

Do not exchange large sums of money in local banks, unless it is very near the hotel. Ask about a deposit box or safe for currency and valuables at the hotel.

课文 2　Text B

Section Ⅰ: Dialog
Interpret the following dialog alternatively into English and Chinese.

客人: Excuse me, sir.

服务人员：请问，夫人，您有什么事？

客人：You know, I'm going back to the United States the day after tomorrow. So I'd like to convert the unused Renmimbi back to US dollar. Is that all right?

服务人员：可以，夫人。

客人：Good. Here's the money.

服务人员：多少？我数一下。12张100元的，……3张50元的，……5张10元的，……9张5元的，……12张1元的。一共1457元。

客人：Yes. That's right.

服务人员：今天的汇率是，让我看看啊，100美元兑换688.39元。所以，是211.6533美元。

客人：Thank you.

服务人员：这是您的货币兑换收据。请保管好。

客人：I will.

服务人员：还有什么能为您效劳的吗，夫人？

客人：Yes. You see, I'm going back to the United States via Seoul. And I'm going to stay there for a couple of days. I know I can change some money at the airport. But I think it's handy for me to have some Korean Won with me.

服务人员：没错，夫人。所以，您想兑换一些韩元？

客人：Yes. I have 500 yuan here.

服务人员：您想要什么面值的，夫人？

客人：In smaller bills, please.

服务人员：好的。今天人民币对韩元的汇率是1元兑换170.0054韩元。所以是85002.7韩元。您看，我给您85张1000元的，其余的是硬币，行吗？

客人：Very good, sir.

服务人员：好的。这是您的钱。您知道吗，夫人，我们希望能很快再次接待您。

客人：That's very nice of you to say so.

服务人员：旅途平安，夫人。

客人：Thank you. Your remarks have made me feel more at home. Hope to see you again soon. Goodbye.

服务人员：再见。

Section Ⅱ: Passage

Interpret the following passage into Chinese.

Visa, MasterCard, AmEx

Credit card companies are like watches. As long as they work, you don't worry much how.

That said, their inner mechanisms may differ markedly. Now we are going to have a close look at the three major credit cards in America and the world as a whole, their histories and other distinctive features.

Visa and MasterCard do not issue cards. Rather, they function as intermediary organizations creating networks between financial companies, including major banks and credit unions that issue cards bearing the Visa or MasterCard name, and merchants providing goods and services. Visa and MasterCard set and maintain rules governing use of their branded cards.

When a cardholder requests a purchase via either Visa or MasterCard, it triggers a multistep process. The merchant submits the charge to his or her bank, which requests authorization from the issuer of the card. If there are enough funds available in the cardholder's account, the issuer, and subsequently the merchant's bank, can authorize the transaction.

At the end of a business day, a merchant sends a batch of sales receipts to its bank, which distributes them to the appropriate issuing organizations. For example, the merchant's bank will send separate batches to Chase, Bank of America or Barclays.

Each issuer subtracts a fee from the amount charged. The issuer shares this fee with Visa or MasterCard. The card network sends the remaining amount to the merchant's bank, which subtracts its own fee before advancing a final total to the merchant.

Both cards may be used at more than 25 million locations in 170 countries.

Whereas the Visa and MasterCard systems engage many organizations, American Express is akin to one-stop shops. That is, it issues its own cards, authorize purchases and settle both with consumers and merchants.

American Express's roots date to the mid-19th century when the company was a competitor to the U. S. Postal Service. It invented traveler's checks in 1891 but didn't enter the credit card business until the late 1950s when it introduced a charge card for travel and entertainment expenses. However, it didn't allow revolving payments until 1987; prior to then, it required customers to pay their balance in full at the end of each month.

American Express generally charges merchants a higher fee. That may account for its lesser reach than Visa and MasterCard. American Express says its cards are accepted in more than 130 countries.

Section Ⅲ：Passage
Interpret the following passage into English.

人民币的币种

　　中国的货币叫作"人民币"，简称"元"，意思是"人民的货币"。人民币有3种单位：元、角、分。人民币是中华人民共和国境内唯一通用的货币。在中国旅游的外国人必须清楚，在边远地区不能使用信用卡，也不能使用旅行支票。所以，要随身携带足够的现金，用以支付各种费用。你可以很方便地把自己随身携带的货币兑换成人民币，但是，你需要出具收据，方可在旅行结束时把没有用完的人民币兑回原来的币种。

　　元

　　人民币主要是纸币。目前流通的有新版的，也有旧版的。所以，你在支付时要看看是什么版的，在拿到找零时也要看看是什么版的，这一点很重要。旧版上印的通常是工人或少数民族的图像。新版上印的是毛主席的头像，面额在纸币中间，用阿拉伯数字写出，很醒目。最大的面值是100元，所以，用现金购买贵重物品时，需要一大沓钱。人民币的面额有100元、50元、20元、10元、5元和1元。还有1元的硬币。要仔细区别这些纸币，以免结账时弄混了。

　　角

　　一角等于十分之一元。角的面值有5角和1角。新版5角硬币是金色的，旧版是铜色的。1角硬币很小，是银白色的，圆的，中间有一个很大的数字1。角常被误当成元，所以，要注意二者之间的区别。

　　分

　　分是一百分之一元，十分之一角。分不是很有用，对于城市居民或游客来说，几乎没有任何购买力。如今，5分硬币、2分纸币、1分纸币和1分硬币已经或逐渐退出历史舞台。

参考答案

Section Ⅰ：Dialog

　　客人：打扰了，先生。
　　服务人员：Yes，ma'am?
　　客人：你知道，我后天返回美国。所以，想把没用完的人民币兑换回美元。可以吗？
　　服务人员：Yes，ma'am.

客人：好。这是我的钱。

服务人员：How much? Let me count. Twelve 100s, ... three 50s, ... five 10s, ... nine 5s and ... twelve 1s. That's 1,457 yuan in total.

客人：是的。没错。

服务人员：The exchange rate today is, let me see, 688.39 yuan for 100 US dollars So you get 211.6533 dollars.

客人：谢谢。

服务人员：Here is the currency exchange receipt. Be sure to keep it.

客人：我会的。

服务人员：Anything else I can do for you, ma'am?

客人：有的。你看，我经过首尔回美国，想在那里待上几天。我知道，可以在机场兑换货币，但是，我想身上带一些韩元还是很方便的。

服务人员：Yes, ma'am. So you want to change some money into Korean Won?

客人：是的。我这里有500元人民币。

服务人员：In what denominations do you prefer, ma'am?

客人：小面额的。

服务人员：OK. The exchange rate between Won and yuan today is 170.0054 Won for 1 yuan. So you get 85,002.7 Won. How about I give you eighty-five 1000s, and the rest in coins?

客人：很好，先生。

服务人员：OK. Here's your money. You know what, ma'am? We are looking forward to hosting you again soon.

客人：您这么说，我很高兴。

服务人员：Have a safe trip home, ma'am.

客人：谢谢。你的话让我更有一种宾至如归的感觉。希望很快能再次见到你。再见。

服务人员：Bye.

Section Ⅱ： Passage

维萨、万事达和美国运通

信用卡公司就像手表一样，只要正常运行，就不必太关心其工作原理。

话虽如此，它们的内在机制可能千差万别。现在，让我们好好看看美国乃至整个世界的三大主要信用卡的历史及其各自的特色。

维萨和万事达本身不发行信用卡。它们作为中介机构，在包括主要银行在内的金融公司、发行维萨和万事达卡的信用合作社以及提供商品和服务的商号之间架起桥梁。维萨和万事达制定规则，维护规则，管理其品牌的使用。

当持卡人使用维萨卡或万事达卡支付时，便激活了一个多步过程。商号把顾客消费金额提交给其所在的银行，请求发行人授权。如果持卡人账户内有足够的资金，发行人和商号所在的银行可以授权交易。

在交易日的最后，商号把一大批销售收据发送给其所在的银行，银行把它们分别发送到相关的发行机构。比如，商号所在的银行将把这些收据分发到美国运通、美国银行或巴克莱银行。

每个发行机构都从消费额中收取一定的费用，与维萨或万事达共享。信用卡网络把剩余的金额发送到商户所在的银行，银行减去自己的费用之后，把最终的余额发送给商户。

维萨卡和万事达卡可以在170个国家的2500万个地点使用。

维萨和万事达系统涉及许多机构，而美国运通类似一站式商店。也就是说，它自己发行信用卡，自己授权购买，分别与消费者和商号结算。

美国运通的起源可以追溯到19世纪中叶，当时，它是美国邮政服务的竞争对手。它在1891年发明了旅行支票，但直到20世纪50年代末才进入信用卡业务。那时，它推出了一种签账卡，用于支付旅行和娱乐费用。然而，美国运通直到1987年才允许按循环账户进行支付；之前，要求客户在每月月底还清信用卡债务。

美国运通一般对商户收取更高的费用，这可能就是它没有维萨卡和万事达卡普及的原因。美国运通表示，他们的信用卡可以在130多个国家使用。

Section Ⅲ: Passage

Types of Money in China

Chinese money is called *Renminbi* (abbreviated as RMB, which means "the people's money") and is denominated in three types: *yuan*, *jiao* and *fen*. Chinese currency is the only money accepted in the People's Republic of China and foreigners traveling in China should be aware that outlying areas will not take credit cards and may not accept traveler's checks either. So it is prudent to carry enough cash to pay your way. You may freely exchange your currency to Chinese money but you will need your receipt to change any unspent monies back at the end of your trip.

Yuan

The *yuan* is primarily paper money. There are old and new bills in circulation so it is important to pay attention to what you give as payment and what you receive as change. Older bills generally have pictures of workers or ethnic groups on them. Newer bills have a picture of Chairman Mao on them and the denomination is prominently displayed in Arabic numerals in the center of the bill. The highest denomination is 100 *yuan* so, if you are buying something expensive in cash, you will need a sack of bills to complete the transaction. Yuan bills come in values of 100, 50, 20, 10, 5, and 1 RMB. There is also a silver 1 *yuan* coin. Take note of the differences between these bills to avoid confusion when paying merchants.

Jiao

One *jiao* is worth one-tenth of a *yuan*. *Jiao* comes in denominations of 5, and 1. The 5 *jiao* coins are gold-colored, while the old ones were bronze-colored. The 1 *jiao* coins are small—a silver-colored one is round and displays a large, centered 1. *Jiao* is most commonly mistaken for *yuan* so take note of the differences between the two.

Fen

Fen is worth one-hundredth of a *yuan*, one-tenth of a *jiao*. Fen isn't very useful because it has almost no buying power for a city dweller or tourist. The 5 *fen* coin, 2 *fen* bill, 2 *fen* coin, 1 *fen* bill, and 1 *fen* coin have or gradually faded into the archives of RMB history.

第8单元
购物中心

At the Store

Text A

Section Ⅰ: Dialog
Interpret the following dialog alternatively into English and Chinese.

售货员：Hello, sir. Can I help you?

客人：我对中国书法很感兴趣，我来看看能否淘点什么特别的宝贝。

售货员：You have come to the right place, sir. I myself am a great fan of calligraphy as I was born into a calligrapher's family.

客人：太好了。来到你的店里，似乎踏上了寻宝之旅。

售货员：What do you have in mind, sir?

客人：没有什么固定目标。实际上，说到书法，我是个外行。我是3年前上中国文化课时才开始接触书法的。

售货员：That explains it. So you have a general knowledge of Chinese calligraphy.

客人：不能那么说。应该说，只知道点皮毛而已。我知道，书法在中国以及包括日本、韩国、越南在内的东方国家是一门艺术。

售货员：You are being modest. Just look around. If you have any questions, don't hesitate to ask.

客人：好的。我认识"马"字。旁边那些字是什么？

售货员：Actually, they are the same character written in different styles. Look, this is in oracle script; this is in bronze script; this is in seal script; this is in cursive script; this is in clerical or official script; and this is in regular script.

客人：你真是行家啊！我只知道楷书和隶书。

售货员：We also have some well-known traditional Chinese paintings here.

客人：我一进门就注意到了。我们西方有油画，但国内很难见到中国国画。我想，送我表妹很合适。她目前是一名艺术生，辅修西方油画。

售货员：Generally speaking, traditional Chinese paintings fall into 2 major schools, fine brushwork paintings, and freehand brushwork paintings.

客人：明白了。

售货员：These are landscape paintings, these are bird-and-flower paintings, and these are figure paintings.

客人：我喜欢风景画。你这里有什么好的吗？

售货员：How about this one? It is the work of one of the best painters in China.

客人：长城。好的。我去年夏天去过。

售货员：And this one? This is the Huangshan Mountain, one of the top 5 mountains in China.

客人：很雄伟。好的，这两幅我都要了。另外，我还想要一幅书法作品。

售货员：What do you think of this one? Shou, meaning long life.

客人：很好。要了。我要送给我爸爸，作为他60大寿的礼物。

售货员：You thought of everything.

客人：请给我分开包装。

售货员：No problem. We have special gift boxes.

客人：好的。一共多少钱？

售货员：4800 yuan.

客人：能便宜点吗？

售货员：Sorry, sir, it's one price for all, in principle.

客人：你的意思是不二价？

售货员：In principle, yes. However, as you are a great fan of Chinese culture, and as the piece of calligraphy you chose happens to be one of my works, I'll give it to you as a gift and as a gesture of my good will. So, altogether it's 4300 yuan.

客人：噢，谢谢。真不敢相信自己的耳朵。真是上天所赐啊。我发财了。给你钱。

售货员：Thanks. Please bring your friends along with you next time you come.

客人：会的，会的。再次感谢。再见。

售货员：Bye.

Section Ⅱ: Passage
Interpret the following passage into Chinese.

Pros and Cons of Hotel Mini Bars

Like anything, Mini Bars or Mini Marts in hotels are a mixed blessing for those parents traveling with children.

Convenience

There is no doubt that having a Mini Mart in your room is much preferable to going out in an unfamiliar neighborhood at late night to satisfy a craving for something. It is convenience that is being sold to the patron, not price.

The saving of time over money is the goal because, while there may be a 7-Eleven or other similar Mini Mart somewhere near the hotel it might involve getting lost, or worse still, getting back the goodies, wet and cold, if the weather is not nice.

The other side is that while being convenient, it is also expensive. A small bag of chips is much more than it would cost at a 7-Eleven (let alone a grocery store), and bottles of soda or water are often two or three times the cost of a gallon of gasoline.

Satisfying

The satisfaction argument can be used in that salt and sugar are usually very satisfying treats. The children will eat away and peace can be achieved, for a moment at least, until the sugar hits and the little ones begin to bounce off walls.

The short-term peace versus the long-term damage to the sleep of the family (let alone the unfortunate neighboring guests) might also be seen as longer-term damage to the children's health.

The snacks contained in the Mini Bar are nutritionally a disaster. Calling them "processed food" is almost an insult to processed food as they are mostly sugars, salts and various chemicals.

Vacation Rules

The argument that "vacation rules" means less strict diets can also be used by the parent.

Going with the flow of the vacation can mean less restrictive diets for the children who do not have dietary restrictions. More chips and soda for a week or a few days may not destroy a child's life.

The other side of the argument is that the children might be exposed to ingredients not in their normal at-home diet and could experience some issues with these new foods. Children could get hives or worse reactions to snack foods that might add a touch of misery to an otherwise nice family vacation.

Unwanted Temptation

Parents who do not want their younger children sampling alcohol before a certain age may want to specifically prohibit the children from opening certain items on the beverage shelf. The price of allowing this to happen is astronomical, not merely in the inflated prices of the alcohol itself, but in later long-term problems with the children.

Conclusions

Mini Bars offer convenience at a large price.

They offer satisfying, if unhealthy, choices for a quick snack or even a meal substitute.

They offer temptation in the form of forbidden fruit but also a teachable moment for the parent who wishes to explain why alcohol is not appropriate for children.

Another conclusion is that even the snack and soda dispensers on the hotel floors by the ice machines offer a cheaper alternative to the Mini Bar.

And with a bit of planning, a trip can be made to a local grocery store to secure healthier snacks, fruit and drinks for a family that are also a cheaper alternative to the delicious but malevolent treats in the room's Mini Bar.

Section Ⅲ: Passage
Interpret the following passage into English.

如何增加酒店收入

酒店业是一个竞争激烈的行业，因此，酒店必须不断寻找新的方法，提高自身的产品和服务质量，保持经济上能正常运转。除了提供一流的服务水平、一流的住宿条件以外，精干的酒店经理也会寻找其他途径，提供配套产品和增值服务，增加酒店的收入。

一、瞄准当地的利基市场。例如，如果酒店坐落在机场附近，可以通过对商务旅行者的营销增加收入；如果酒店接近像主题公园这样的家庭旅游目的地，可以把目标聚焦在年轻家庭和孩子身上。根据人口情况进行营销，可以引来更多的顾客，增加收入。

二、对客人进行调查，了解他们颇感兴趣、愿意购买的产品和服务。例如，如果酒店客人经常询问就餐事宜，如果店内没有餐厅或者送餐服务，那么，不妨考虑在这些方面进行投资，增加未来的收入。如果商务旅行者提出诸如租赁笔记本电脑或使用商务中心这样的要求，可以考虑添加这些设施，通过收取使用费增加收入。

三、增加娱乐设施，收取相应费用。例如，酒吧里可以增加"大众麦克风"或乐队演出夜场，会议中心可以增加电影放映。

四、扩大礼品店经营范围，出售地方产品、纪念品、服装、食品和饮料。

五、追加销售便利设施。如果酒店服务项目很多，可推出一系列"一揽子协议"，通过追加销售的方式增加收入。例如，出售健身卡、游泳卡或商务中心卡，增加收入；提供灵活的入住和退房时间，额外收费。优先停车或日常洗衣服务等升级项目也可以考虑在内。

六、与其他公司合作。例如，可以与汽车服务公司或豪华轿车公司签订合同，为客人提供私人交通工具，同时，赚取推介费。

七、在网上进行特价推销，通过电子邮件和社交媒体营销。为客人提供免费网络服务，鼓励客人发微博或发帖及时更新住店期间的状态和照片。

八、紧密跟踪竞争对手，了解最新动态，并相应调整酒店的成本和服务。例如，推出与竞争对手相对应的价格，为回头客提供特价或升级服务。

参考答案

Section Ⅰ : Dialog

售货员：先生，您好。您要买点什么？

客人：I'm interested in Chinese calligraphy. I'm here to see if I can pick up something nice and special.

售货员：您算来对地方了，先生。我本人就很喜欢书法，我就出生在一个书法家的家庭。

客人：Awesome. It seems like I am on a treasure-hunting trip in your store.

售货员：先生，您有什么固定目标吗？

客人：Nothing in particular. Actually, when it comes to calligraphy, I'm a layman. I came into contact with calligraphy when I attended a Chinese culture class 3 years ago.

售货员：原来如此。这么说，您对书法有一定的了解了。

客人：Not really. Just a smattering of knowledge of it, I should say. I know calligraphy is an art in China and some countries in the East, like Japan, Korea and Vietnam.

售货员：您谦虚了。随便看吧。有问题，尽管问。

客人：OK. I know the character *ma*, meaning *horse*. What are the other characters beside it?

售货员：实际上，是同一个字，只是风格不同而已。看，这是甲骨文；这是金文；这是篆书；这是草书；这是隶书；这是楷书。

客人：You really know your stuff. I know regular script and official script only.

售货员：我们这里还有一些著名的国画。

客人：I noticed that the moment I came in. We have oil paintings in the West. We can hardly find traditional Chinese paintings back home. I think they will make very good gifts for my cousin. She is currently an art student, minoring in Western oil paintings.

售货员：一般来说，国画分为两种：工笔和写意。

客人：I see.

售货员：这些是山水画，这些是花鸟画，这些是人物画。

客人：I prefer landscape paintings. What do you recommend?

售货员：这一幅怎么样？ 它是中国杰出画家的作品。

客人：The Great Wall. Good. I was there last summer.

售货员：这一幅呢？ 这是黄山，中国的五岳之一。

客人：Impressive. OK. I'll take these two. Besides, I'd also like a piece of calligraphy.

售货员：这一幅您觉得怎么样？"寿"字，意思是"长命百岁"。

客人：That's great. I'll take it. I'll give it to my dad as his 60th birthday gift.

售货员：您想得真周到啊。

客人：Will you wrap them up separately, please?

售货员：没问题。我们有特制的礼品盒。

客人：Good. How much altogether?

售货员：4800元。

客人：Can you come down a little?

售货员：对不起，先生，我们原则上一口价。

客人：No second price, you mean?

售货员：原则上，是的。不过，由于您酷爱中国文化，加上您刚才选的这幅书法是我的作品，我打算把它送给您，略表心意。这样，一共4300元。

客人：Oh, thank you. I couldn't believe my ears. It's a godsend. I just got a windfall. Here's the money.

售货员：谢谢。下次来，请把朋友一起带来。

客人：I will. I will. Thanks again. Goodbye.

售货员：再见。

Section II: Passage

酒店迷你酒吧的利弊

跟任何东西一样，酒店里的"迷你酒吧"或"迷你超市"，对带孩子一起旅行的父母来说，是一件喜忧参半的事情。

方便

毫无疑问，房间里有个"迷你超市"，远比在深更半夜到陌生小区购买东西更受欢迎。这里，出售给顾客的是方便，与价格无关。

人们的目标是节省时间，而非金钱，这是因为，虽然旅馆附近可能会有7-11或其他类似的"迷你超市"，但是，你可能会迷路，更有甚者，如果赶上坏天气，买回来的好吃的东西可能会变得潮乎乎的、冷冰冰的。

另一方面，虽然方便，价格也不菲啊。一小袋薯片的价格远远高于7-11，更不用说杂货店了，瓶装苏打水、普通瓶装水的价格通常是一加仑汽油的两三倍。

满意

说到满意，主要表现在盐糖通常是非常令人满意的"美食"。孩子们可以尽情地吃，短期内不会发生"战争"。不过，过不了多久，吃下去的糖开始发挥威力，小家伙们便开始变得兴奋异常。

为了短期和平，牺牲睡眠对全家（更不用说对周边不幸的客人）造成的长期伤害，以及对儿童本身健康的危害也不是一两天就可以消除的。迷你酒吧里的零食，从营养的角度来说，就是一个灾难。说它们是"加工食品"几乎就是对"加工食品"的侮辱，因为它们的成分大多是糖、盐和各种各样的化学物质。

休假制度

有人说，休假制度意味着不必遵守严格的饮食习惯，这一点父母也可以参考。

外出度假意味着，对于没有饮食限制的孩子来说，可以放开进食。一周内或几天内多吃几包薯片、多喝几瓶苏打水，要不了孩子的命。

另一方面，有人认为，孩子们可能会接触一些平时家庭菜谱里没有的东西，而这些新的食物可能会给孩子带来健康问题。孩子可能会得荨麻疹，或者，更糟糕的是，对零食的不良反应可能会给原本愉快的家庭旅行带来一丝痛苦。

不必要的诱惑

不希望孩子在一定年龄前接触烈酒的父母，可能会明确禁止孩子打开货架上的某些饮品。否则，代价会非常巨大。这不仅表现在烈酒本身的价格上，而且，还表现在酒精对孩子日后成长的长期影响上。

结论

迷你酒吧提供便利，但价格也贵。

它们为客人提供令人满意的选择，可以吃快餐，也可以吃一日三餐的替代品，只是对健康不利。

它们以"禁果"的形式提供诱惑，也给父母提供了一个教育孩子的机会，告诉孩子为什么酒精对他们不好。

另一个结论是，即便是酒店楼层制冰机旁边的零食和苏打水售货机里的商品也比迷你酒吧里的便宜。

稍加计划，就可以去当地的杂货店为全家购买健康的零食、水果和饮料，那也比房间中迷你酒吧里可口但可怕的"美食"来得便宜。

Section Ⅲ: Passage

How to Increase Revenue in Hotels

As they operate in a competitive industry, hotels must continually look for ways to augment their products and services to remain financially viable. In addition to providing superior levels of service and top-notch accommodations, savvy hotel managers also look for ways to increase revenue by offering ancillary products and services that add value to the customer experience.

1. Target niche markets that make sense for your particular location. For example, a hotel located near the airport might increase revenue by marketing to business travelers, while hotels close to family destination locations, like theme parks, could target young families and children. Marketing to select demographics can bring in more customers and increase revenue.

2. Survey guests to learn more about products and services they find attractive and would be willing to pay for. For example, if hotel guests regularly ask about dining options, and you have no in-hotel restaurant or room service options, consider investing in these upgrades as a way to generate future revenue. If business travelers request services such as laptop rentals or a business service center, consider adding these amenities as a way to increase revenue through usage surcharges.

3. Add entertainment options and charge a fee. For example, you might add an open-mic or band night in the bar or a movie screening in a conference center.

4. Expand gift shop offering to include locally-made items, souvenirs, clothing items and food and drinks.

5. Up-sell amenities. If you have a wide range of services available in your hotel, offer package deals that allow you to up-sell or upgrade your customers as a way of increasing revenue. For example, sell a pass for your fitness center, swimming pool or business services center as an extra upgrade, or provide flexible check-in and check-out times for an additional surcharge. Consider other upgraded options like preferred parking or daily laundry service.

6. Partner with other companies. For example, you might contract with a car service or limousine company that can provide guests with private transportation while giving you a referral payment.

7. Promote specials online and through email and social media marketing. Offer hotel guests free Internet access and encourage them to blog or post status updates and photos related to their stay at your property.

8. Keep track of what your competition is doing and adjust your costs and services accordingly. For example, offer to match the competition's prices, or offer specials or upgrades to repeat customers.

课文 2　　Text B

Section I: Dialog
Interpret the following dialog alternatively into English and Chinese.

售货员：Hi, ma'am. Is there anything you are particularly interested in here?

客人：我想为家人买点礼物。

售货员：I see. Do you have anything in mind? Or would you like me to recommend something for you?

客人：我想要一些特别的东西，一些具有异国情调的东西。

售货员：I know. How about some key chains? They are very Chinese, and they come in all styles.

客人：这个主意不错。

售货员：See? We have Monkey King, Flying Goddess, Jade Rabbit, Compass, Beijing Opera facial masks, and what not.

客人：嗯，我想我会买几个。

售货员：We also have many kinds of coasters. The while-and-blue porcelain ones are most popular both at home and abroad.

客人：真漂亮！

售货员：Do you like bookmarks? These bookmarks are characters from well-known novels, like *The Story of the Stone*, *Journey to the West*, *Water Margin*, and *Romance of the Three Kingdoms*.

客人：非常特别。

售货员：These are Chinese knots, which can bring you good luck.

客人：以前见过。我知道，红色在中国文化里是幸福吉祥的颜色。

售货员：So you are an old China hand.

客人：过奖了。

售货员：Here are Chinese paper cuts, paperweights, mini-folding-screens, silk fans, fridge magnets, and cloisonné or Beijing enamel, as it is called.

客人：这真是一个中国礼物王国啊！

售货员：Yes. For ladies, we also have different kinds of bracelets and necklaces. And for gentlemen, we have silk neckties, metal name card cases, snuff bottles and the like.

客人：这些是什么？

售货员：They are amulets. They are thought to be a protection against evil.

客人：这些呢？

售货员：Car pendants. Some of them are made of jade, and others, of peach wood.

客人：为什么是桃木？

售货员：Because, like jade, peach wood is believed to have the power to exorcise evil spirits.

客人：是吗？从未听说过。

售货员：Well, have you made up your mind, ma'am?

客人：嗯。我要5个钥匙链、2套青花瓷杯子垫儿、2个中国结、2个手镯、2个项链、1个鼻烟壶、2个桃木汽车挂件，最后，再为我自己买个护身符吧。一共多少钱？

售货员：Just a moment, ma'am. Let me work it out for you. By the way, do you pay by cash or by credit card?

客人：现金。

售货员：In that case, I'll give you a 10% discount. That adds up to 432 yuan. So you have saved 48 yuan.

客人：8折怎么样？

售货员：20% off? I'm afraid you are asking too much, ma'am.

客人：你要是我，也希望有个优惠价格。越便宜越好，对吧？

售货员：I fully understand, ma'am. How about we split the difference and meet each other half way? Say 15%.

客人：我举双手赞成。谢谢。给你钱。

售货员：Thanks. There you go. Goodbye, ma'am.

客人：祝你愉快。

Section Ⅱ: Passage

Interpret the following passage into Chinese.

Sales Strategies for Hotels

Operating a hotel is a difficult way to make a steady profit, with shifting travel and economic trends putting many hotel operators in peril. However, successful sales strategies can keep your hotel bringing in customers consistently. Hotel sales require knowing what guests want and working to earn their trust to secure future sales.

Responding to Customers

Setting up a great hotel is essential to making sales, but keeping it up to guests' standards is equally important. A good sales strategy is to stay attentive to your customers. This means giving guests ample opportunities to leave comments. Leave them an in-room comment card or send them an email survey following their stay. More in-depth surveys via email or telephone might be appropriate for frequent guests, because they could have special insight into your hotel's strengths and weaknesses. You should also scour online reservation sites and message boards to gauge unsolicited customer feedback.

Make improvements to your hotel based upon guest requests. In your advertising, publicize these improvements. Even a simple upgrade to your property could boost sales.

Rewards Programs

It costs five times as much to gain a new hotel sale than to sell to a returning customer, according to the Hotel Marketing Strategies website. To improve your chances for repeat sales, offer a rewards program for frequent guests. Offer special discounts and free room upgrades to guests enrolling in your program or once they reach a certain number of visits. This can instill a sense of loyalty, thereby bringing increased sales at minimal cost to your sales and marketing budget.

Section Ⅲ: Passage
Interpret the following passage into English.

何为顾客满意度

顾客满意度指的是客户是否愿意将来与你或你的公司做生意。顾客满意度涉及诸多因素，包括客户服务、产品质量以及营商便利程度。公司必须把顾客满意度看成是创造客户终身价值的一个重要因素。

可靠的客户服务

酒店应该努力兑现自己的承诺。可靠性是服务质量最重要的方面。可靠性涉及服务质量的一致性和可信性。所以，一开始就要提供优质服务。雇员应该微笑着接电话。微笑是可以"从声音里听出来的"。最让顾客受不了的是，接待他的雇员认为客户是在浪费他的时间。

客户的信心

服务人员应该在客户心里建立信任和信心。这就要求员工知识渊博，彬彬有礼，精明能干。服务人员应该训练有素，能应对突发事件。他们应该经过仔细挑选，接受严格培训，从而确保第一次见面就给客户一个愉快的体验。

产品、服务的价值

顾客满意度在很大程度上取决于顾客以最有竞争力的价格获得了优质产品或优质服务。顾客不仅仅寻求合适的产品或服务，而且还寻求懂产品的人、懂服务的人。

移情性

给顾客个性化的关注。顾客应该感到，他们的需要对酒店很重要。每一位顾客得到的服务都应该是量身定做的。这就要求向员工赋权，给他们一个自由的空间。

快速反应

"服务"的本质是提供现成服务。大多服务都是当着顾客的面现场提供的。顾客需要服务时,马上满足,这一点十分重要。例如,周末提供汽车服务,这极大方便了周末上班的顾客。

客户调查

许多企业发现,了解顾客的满意度很有价值。要及时跟踪顾客的任何问题。通过客户调查,可以很好地发现顾客对新服务、新产品的需求。

客户的终身价值

关注顾客需求是一项很好的投资。史密斯先生会告诉琼斯先生他在酒店里的愉快经历,同样,琼斯先生会告诉格林先生。这样的循环周而复始。而这一切都恰恰始于顾客满意度。

Section Ⅰ: Dialog

售货员:夫人,您好。有特别感兴趣的东西吗?

客人:I'm looking for some gifts for my family.

售货员:知道了。您是想好了呢,还是想让我给您推荐几款?

客人:I want something special, something exotic.

售货员:明白。买些钥匙链怎么样? 很有中国特色,而且,款式齐全。

客人:That's a good idea.

售货员:看到了吧? 有美猴王、飞天、玉兔、指南针、脸谱等。

客人:Yes. I think I'll take some.

售货员:还有很多种杯子垫儿。这些青花瓷的在国内外都很流行。

客人:How beautiful!

售货员:您喜欢书签吗? 这些书签都是著名小说里的人物,如《红楼梦》《西游记》《水浒》《三国演义》等。

客人:Very unique.

售货员:这些是中国结,它们会给您带来好运。

客人:I've seen them before. I know, red is the color of happiness and auspiciousness in Chinese culture.

售货员:看来,您是中国通。

客人:You flatter me.

售货员:这是中国剪纸、镇纸、小屏风、绢扇、冰箱贴、景泰蓝,景泰蓝又叫北京珐琅等。

客人：This is really a kingdom of Chinese gifts.

售货员：是啊。对女士来说，我们还有各种各样的手镯和项链。对男士来说，我们有丝绸领带、金属名片盒、鼻烟壶等。

客人：What are these?

售货员：是护身符。都说，可以驱鬼辟邪。

客人：And these?

售货员：汽车挂件。有玉石的，有桃木的。

客人：Why peach wood ?

售货员：因为，和玉石一样，桃木据说可以驱走恶魔。

客人：Really? I've never heard of that before.

售货员：嗯，夫人，您拿定主意了吗？

客人：Yes. I'd like 5 key chains, 2 sets of while-and-blue porcelain coasters, 2 Chinese knots, 2 bracelets, 2 necklaces, 1 snuff bottle, 2 peach wood car pendants, and finally, 1 amulet for myself. How much?

售货员：请稍等，夫人。我给您算一下。对了，您是现金结账，还是刷卡？

客人：By cash.

售货员：那样的话，我给您打个9折。这样，一共是432元。您省了48元。

客人：How about 20% off?

售货员：8折？ 恐怕您是狮子大开口了，夫人。

客人：If you were in my shoes, you'd also like to have a better price. The cheaper, the better. Right?

售货员：我完全理解，夫人。要不我们抛开分歧，各让一步，如何？ 比如说，8.5折?

客人：I couldn't agree more. Thank you. Here's the money.

售货员：谢谢。您拿好了。再见，夫人。

客人：Have a great day.

Section Ⅱ： Passage

酒店销售策略

经营酒店很难确保稳定的利润，这是因为旅游和经济趋势的不断变化把许多酒店经营者推向了危险境地。然而，成功的销售策略可以让酒店的客户源源不断。酒店销售需要了解客人的需求，需要努力赢得他们的信任，才能确保未来的销售。

应对客户

建造一个高档酒店对销售来说至关重要，但达到客人的要求同样重要。一个良好的销售策略就是要保持对客户的关注，这意味着给客人提供大量的留言机会。在客房里留一张"留言卡",或者在客人离店后通过电子邮件进行跟踪调查。对于常客来说,通过电子邮件或电话进行更深入的调查比较合适,因为他们对酒店的优势和劣势会有特殊的洞察力。你也应该搜索在线预订网站和留言板,对不请自来的客户反馈进行判断评估。

根据客人的要求,对酒店服务进行改进。在广告中,把改进的地方加进去。即使是一个简单的升级,也可能会提振销售。

奖励计划

根据酒店营销策略网站的统计,要拓展一个新的销售渠道,其成本是老客户的5倍。为了提高对老客户的销售率,应该推出一个常客奖励计划。对于加入该计划的客户,或者达到一定入住次数的客户,为他们提供特别折扣和免费房间升级。这可以培养客户的忠诚度,从而以最小的成本增加你的销售和营销预算。

Section Ⅲ: Passage

What Defines Customer Satisfaction?

Customer satisfaction is defined by whether the customer chooses to do business with you or your company in the future. Many factors play a role in customer satisfaction, including customer service, product quality and the ease of doing business. Companies must consider customer satisfaction as an important role in the lifetime value of a customer.

Reliable Customer Service

Hotels should strive to deliver on their promises. Reliability is the most important dimension of service quality. It involves both consistency in quality and dependability. Provide the service right the first time. Employees should answer the phone with a smile. A smile can be "heard in someone's voice". Nothing frustrates customers more than being served by an employee who feels the customer is a waste of their time.

Customer Confidence

Service employees should create trust and confidence in the customer. This requires being knowledgeable, courteous and competent. Service employees should be well trained to meet contingencies. They should be subject to careful selection and grooming to ensure a pleasant encounter for the customer.

The Value of Products and Services

Customer satisfaction depends greatly upon receiving a quality product or service at a competitive price. Not only is the customer looking for the right product or service, he is looking for someone who is knowledgeable about the product or service as well.

Empathy with the Customer

Give personalized attention to the customer. Customers should feel that their needs are important to the organization. The service provided to each customer should be customized to her specific needs. This requires employee empowerment and leeway.

Responsiveness and Promptness

The nature of "service" precludes serving it off the shelf. Most types of services are produced and delivered there and then in the presence of the customer. It is important to deliver the service when the customer requires it. For example, providing car services at the weekend is convenient for the working customer.

Customer Surveys

Many businesses have found value in surveying customers about satisfaction. Follow up with any concerns or issues the customer addresses. Customer surveys are an excellent way to discover new services or products customers want.

The Lifetime Value of a Customer

Focusing on the needs of the customer is a good investment. Mr. Smith will tell Mr. Jones of the pleasant experience he had staying in a hotel. Mr. Jones will then tell Mr. Green, and the cycle continues. It all starts with customer satisfaction.

第9单元
美容美发

At the Beauty Salon

课文 1　　**Text A**

Section Ⅰ: Dialog
Interpret the following dialog alternatively into English and Chinese.

店员: Good afternoon, sir. What can I do for you?
客人: 你好。请给我稍微修一下。
店员: All right. Let's start off by washing your hair?
客人: 好的。
店员: Are you a member of our club or just a guest staying at the hotel?
客人: 我是店里的客人,小姐。
店员: I see. Your hair is good. ...OK, done. Now go back to your seat, please.
客人: 椅子很舒服。我很喜欢这里的环境。
店员: That's good to hear. You mean I just trim it, sir?
客人: 是的。上面去一点,后面短一点,不过,别太短了。
店员: OK. How about the sideburns?
客人: 鬓角请别动,保持原样。
店员: OK. No problem. You do have lots of hair, sir. Would you like me to thin it out a little bit?
客人: 好的,请吧。
店员: That's it. Now your hair is much more manageable.
客人: 是的,没错。对了,请给我刮个脸。
店员: That will surely make you look much better. Younger, I mean.
客人: 是的,我夫人经常说,刮了胡子,我就年轻10岁了。
店员: Yes, beards make men look older, but more sexy.
客人: 您真会说话。
店员: OK. Open your eyes, sir, and look into the mirror. How do you like it?
客人: 总的来说,很不错。可是,……嗯,……太阳穴这儿还是去一点吧。
店员: A little off the temples. ... OK. Now have a look, please. Is it all right, sir?
客人: 嗯,非常好。
店员: Now I'll give you a shampoo before I blow dry your hair.
客人: 好的。
店员: All right, sir, would you like me to use some hairspray or mousse?

客人：啫喱吧。
店员：Gel? OK. We have a very good brand here. Schwarzkopf. Look, it says "This gel's hold is no joke! So put it down and slowly back away if you are not up for the strongest gel hold ever!"
客人：好大的口气啊！
店员：It's non-sticky, no flakes, crazy hold. You want to try that, sir?
客人：好啊。
店员：All right. Is that satisfactory?
客人：嗯，谢谢。
店员：Anything else I can do for you, sir?
客人：没有了，小姐，谢谢。多少钱？
店员：45 yuan.
客人：给你50，不用找了。
店员：Thank you, sir.
客人：再见。

Section II: Passage
Interpret the following passage into Chinese.

Safety and Security Rules for Hotel Management

The two primary goals of hotels to make guests comfortable and to keep them safe are at cross purposes. Hotels need to implement safety and security measures without making guests feel uneasy. "Cornell Hotel & Restaurant Administration Quarterly" found that hotel guests did not appreciate the use of metal detectors, the obvious presence of armed guards, and checking guest identification documents against law enforcement records. In the hospitality industry, security is a delicate balancing act.

Personal Safety

Personal safety should be a key concern for hotels and there are many things to consider. Card key locks are essential for hotels. The card key is assigned to a room from check in and automatically expires at a specific time, regardless of check-out. Smoke and carbon dioxide detectors, fire extinguishers, emergency telephones and emergency exits are all very important in ensuring the safety of guests. The hotel staff should be equipped with evacuation plans, first aid kits and breathing assistance, such as a respirator, in case of an emergency.

Pool and Spa Regulations

Pools and spas should have lifeguards. However, most do not. Hotels with pools should enforce pool hours and hotel staff should be trained in CPR and first aid. Hotel guests should be the only ones with access to the pool and spa facilities. Entrance to the facilities should require activated room card keys.

Surveillance

Video surveillance in public areas around the hotel, monitored by a front desk employee or a security officer, is a cost-effective way to keep track of what is happening on the premises. The presence of closed-circuit television security cameras in plain sight around the hotel acts as a deterrent and gives guests an additional sense of security.

Human surveillance is still an effective way to make the hotel safer. Many hotels employ security personnel to act as bellhops and doormen, securing the perimeter of the hotel and providing an early warning system for suspicious behavior.

Staff Training

Every hotel should train its personnel on how to identify risky situations and how to get help when they think a dangerous situation may be imminent. Hotel staff should also be trained in emergency evacuation procedures. Hotels should conduct drills and simulations to test their emergency plans.

Information Sharing

Hotel management should share information with law enforcement and first responders in advance of any problem. The fire department should have a copy of the hotel floor plans in case of emergency, and law enforcement should alert hotel management of general security alerts such as warnings of terrorist activity.

Safety Design

Good design can help keep hotels safe. The hotel should be set back from the street, with driveways and parking garages located well away from guest rooms. Lobby windows should be protected with bulletproof glass. Hotel key cards should be keyed only to the floor where the guest's room is located. Guests on the 16th floor, for example, should not be able to press an elevator button that lets them stop on the 14th floor.

Section Ⅲ: Passage
Interpret the following passage into English.

美容沙龙

美容沙龙,对很多女性,甚至是一些男人来说,是一个神奇的地方。在美容沙龙里，顾客得到悉心照顾，变得漂漂亮亮。理发、发型设计、美甲、化妆小窍门，甚至还有水疗，这一切都使得美容沙龙成为美丽的诞生地。顾客满意度是美容沙龙业务发展的关键，它可以保证顾客再次回来。

功能

美容沙龙是美丽诞生的地方，也是出售美容产品的地方。美容沙龙有很多名字，如美容院、美容室和美容店等。在美容沙龙里，无论男性美容，还是女性美容，都是靠注册美容师、专业按摩师和注册发型师来完成的。

类型

美容沙龙的营业范围，从局部美容到全身美容，应有尽有。高级美容沙龙大都包括客户所需要的所有护理项目，如美肤、美发、美甲等。有的美容沙龙包括按摩疗法、面部治疗、化妆品的使用、晒黑、脱毛、美甲、修脚、护发等。也有一些美容沙龙已开始提供特色服务，如身体磨砂、洗浴、永久化妆等。

特点

顾客去美容沙龙，希望得到自己想要的护理项目。每个项目都有顾客想要的特点。按摩的特点，是通过触摸皮肤（有时也借助美容产品）让顾客放松，增进健康。修甲修脚是对手脚进行护理，包括手部按摩、足部按摩及软化皮肤等。面部护理是美容沙龙的最大特点之一，不同类型的皮肤及皮肤问题有着不同的护理方法。

注意事项

去美容沙龙院之前，重要的是要考虑一下护理成本，并提前咨询一下专业人士。咨询能让顾客与未来的护理师见面，并了解具体细节。如果顾客皮肤比较敏感或容易过敏，需要根据这种情况制定专门的护理方案。

益处

去美容沙龙有很多益处。身体放松、健康的光泽和友好的气氛是美容沙龙给顾客带来的次要益处。主要的益处在于通过美容满足顾客的需求，缓解压力和紧张情绪。此外，为了满足顾客的美丽需求，还特意配备了专业人员。

参考答案

Section Ⅰ： Dialog

店员：先生，下午好。请问，怎么理？
客人：Hi. I'd like a trim, please.
店员：好的。那先洗洗头吧。
客人：OK.

店员：您是我们的会员，还是住店的客人？

客人：I'm a guest here, miss.

店员：知道了。您的发质不错。…… 嗯，好了。现在，请回到您的座位上。

客人：I feel comfortable in this chair. I like the environment here very much.

店员：您这样说，我很高兴。您的意思是，稍微修一下，先生？

客人：Yes. Just take a little off the top and cut it short in the back. But please don't make it too short.

店员：好的。那鬓角呢？

客人：Don't touch the sideburns, please. Just leave them as they are.

店员：好的，没问题。先生，您的头发很多啊。要不要给您打薄一点？

客人：Yes, go ahead.

店员：好了。现在，您的头发好打理多了。

客人：Yes, you are right. By the way, I'd like a shave, too.

店员：那看上去就更好了，我的意思是，更年轻了。

客人：Yes, my wife often says that as soon as I shave off my beard, I look 10 years younger.

店员：没错。胡子让男人显得老一些，但也更性感一些。

客人：That's sweet.

店员：好了。睁开眼睛，先生，照照镜子。怎么样？

客人：On the whole, it's very good. But ... well ... could you cut a little off the temples, please?

店员：太阳穴，去一点。…… 好了，请看一下。可以了吗，先生？

客人：Yes, perfect.

店员：现在洗一下，然后吹干。

客人：OK.

店员：好了，先生。要打点发胶，还是摩丝？

客人：I prefer gel.

店员：啫喱？ 好的。我们这里有一个非常好的牌子，叫 Schwarzkopf。看，上面写着："这个啫喱的定型能力可不是吹的。如果您对世界上定型能力最强的啫喱还没有心理准备的话，那就请把它放下，慢慢退去吧！"

客人：They really talk big!

店员：这个啫喱不黏腻，不起白屑，造型持久。想试试吗，先生？

客人：Why not?

店员：好了。满意吗？

客人：Yes, thanks.

店员：还有什么可以为您效劳的吗，先生？

客人：No, miss, thank you. How much is it?

店员：45元。
客人：Here's 50. Keep the change.
店员：谢谢，先生。
客人：Bye.

Section Ⅱ：Passage

酒店管理安全条例

　　酒店有两大主要目标，一是让客人住得舒适，一是确保客人的安全。这两个目标可谓南辕北辙。酒店需要采取安全措施，但不能让客人感到不安。《康奈尔酒店和餐饮管理季刊》发现，酒店客人不喜欢金属探测器，不喜欢看到武装警卫，不喜欢以执法为名检查客人的身份证件。在招待行业，安全是一个很微妙的问题，需要好好平衡。

人身安全

　　人身安全应该是酒店关注的重点，有许多事情需要考虑。房卡门锁至关重要。入住时，拿到房间房卡钥匙，到一定时间自动失效，无论是否退房，都是如此。烟雾和二氧化碳探测器、灭火器、应急电话和紧急出口，这些对确保客人安全都是非常重要的。酒店员工应该配备逃生平面图、急救药箱及辅助呼吸设备，如人工呼吸器等，以防万一。

游泳池和水疗中心规定

　　游泳池和水疗中心应该配备救生员。然而，大多数都没有。有游泳池的酒店应该明确开放时间，酒店员工应该在心肺复苏和急救方面接受培训。只有酒店客人才能使用游泳池和水疗设施。需要有激活的房卡钥匙方可进入。

监控

　　在酒店周边的公共区域安装视频监控，由前台员工或安保人员负责，对酒店发生的事情全程跟踪，这是一个很划算的方式。在酒店周围明显的地方安装闭路电视监控摄像头，能起到一种威慑作用，也让客人感到格外安全。

　　人工监控仍是确保酒店更加安全的一个有效方式。许多酒店雇佣保安人员作为行李员和门童，确保酒店周边的安全。如有可疑行为，可起到早期预警作用。

员工培训

　　每个酒店都应该对员工进行培训，告诉他们如何识别危险情况，如何在危险情况即将来临时获得帮助。酒店员工也应该接受紧急疏散方面的培训。酒店应该进行模拟演练，对其应急计划进行测试。

信息共享

　　酒店管理层在问题出现之前应与执法人员和应急人员分享情报。消防部门应该有一份酒店平面图，以备不时之需。执法人员应该提醒酒店管理层，熟悉常见的安全警报,如反恐警报等。

安全设计

优秀的设计可以确保酒店安全。酒店应该远离马路;车道和停车场应该远离客房。一楼大堂的窗户应该安装防弹玻璃。房卡钥匙应该设计成只能到达客人房间所在的楼层。例如,客人住在16层,按下14层的按钮,但他根本无法停在14层。

Section Ⅲ: Passage

Beauty Salons

Beauty salons are a place of magic for many women and even some men. In a beauty salon, the customer is pampered and made beautiful. Haircuts and styles, nail care, makeup tips and even spa options make a beauty salon the place where beauty happens. Customer satisfaction is key in a beauty salon business so that customers keep coming back.

Function

A beauty salon is just that—a place where beauty treatments take place and products for beautifying are sold. They may be called many things, including a beauty parlor, beauty salon and even beauty shops. Cosmetic treatments for men and women are made available in a beauty salon with certified estheticians, professional massage therapists and certified hairstylists.

Types

Types of treatments found at beauty salons can range from a focus on specific treatments to expansive and include a little bit of everything. Many great beauty salons have everything a customer needs to beautify skin, hair and nails. Some of the types of treatments found at beauty salons may include massage therapies, facial treatments, cosmetic applications, tanning options, waxing options, manicures, pedicures and hair care areas. Some beauty salons have started offering specialty services such as body scrubs, baths and also permanent makeup procedures.

Features

A customer can go to a beauty salon to get the treatment she desires. Each treatment offers features that the customer may seek. The features of a massage are that the skin benefits by being touched (sometimes with beauty products) to promote relaxation and well-being. Manicures and pedicures are for the hands and feet; these treatments may feature hand and foot massages as well as treatments to soften the skin in these areas. Facials are one of the biggest features at beauty salons, because there are many different types for different types of skin and skin-related problems.

Considerations

Before heading to a beauty salon, it is important to consider the cost of treatments and a pre-visit consultation with a certified professional. A pre-visit consultation will let you meet the person who will perform the beauty treatments on you and also give her a chance to go over any specifics you may need. The treatments may need to be tailored to your needs if you have sensitive or allergy-prone skin.

Benefits

There are numerous benefits to going to a beauty salon. Relaxation, a healthy glow and a friendly atmosphere are all secondary benefits that a beauty salon offers customers. The primary benefits include beauty treatments to meet your needs, therapies for stress and tension, and professional staffs that can meet any of your beauty needs.

Text B

Section Ⅰ: Dialog

Interpret the following dialog alternatively into English and Chinese.

店员：Good morning, miss. How can we help you today?

客人：我要做头发。今天怎么这么多人啊？

店员：You see, the Moon Festival is just around the corner. And there's going to be a long weekend. People tend to have their hair done before festivals.

客人：有道理。得等多长时间？

店员：About half an hour.

客人：不会吧。

店员：Well, miss, if you are not in a hurry, I suggest you take a seat over here and have a look at the latest hairstyles in this fashion magazine. You might want a change of style.

客人：我觉得你说的也对。谢谢。

店员：You see, here are various styles-hair bobbed, hair swept back, chaplet style, shoulder-length, hair done in a bun, etc. Have a good look at them and I'll help you pick one later, one that agrees with your skin color, and flatters your face.

客人：选择不少啊！谢谢啦。
店员：Take your time, miss. I'll take care of my customer first.
客人：请吧。
(25分钟后)
店员：Very sorry to have kept you waiting so long, miss. Have you made up your mind yet?
客人：还没有。你有什么建议？
店员：Judging from your skin color, and your features, I guess long hair suits you well.
客人：你的意思是披肩发？
店员：Exactly, miss. What do you say?
客人：我同意。毕竟你是美发师，我相信你的眼光。
店员：Good. And you also want a permanent, right?
客人：是的。
店员：A tight, medium or natural curly permanent?
客人：我要自然卷。
店员：Good. Have you ever had your hair dyed, miss?
客人：染过。
店员：And would you like to have it dyed today, miss?
客人：染。染成金发，可以吗？你知道，我不喜欢老是一个颜色。
店员：Blond? I don't think blond is good for your skin tone. How about red? Red is in fashion this year.
客人：我想，这一次还是不跟潮流了吧。
店员：So you want to be original. That's good. To be young means to be different.
客人：当然。
店员：OK, miss, my assistant will give you a shampoo now. Follow him, please.
客人：谢谢。

Section Ⅱ: Passage
Interpret the following passage into Chinese.

What Is the Philosophy of Customer Service?

There is no single philosophy of customer service that is adopted by all businesses across all industries and services. Rather, there are various sets of practices unified by a belief that customers' satisfaction enhances a business's prospect of achieving its goals. Common patterns, however, offer some basic principles of customer service. The specifics can vary greatly, for example between a financial services company dealing with remote clients and a hotel or restaurant providing face-to-face hospitality to guests. Large corporations may have service teams exclusively devoted to this issue.

Accessibility

The philosophical foundation on which customer service must be based is accessibility. Whether in person, by telephone, or by email, customers must be able to contact staff when assistance is needed, and be sure of a timely response. If employees are unable to assist a customer immediately, whether because of a line at the reception desk or a queue of calls waiting, make some acknowledgment of the waiting customer. Telephone queues are made more bearable by accurate recorded messages. Similarly, if queries or complaints cannot immediately be answered, receipt should be promptly acknowledged.

Accountability

Customers can be frustrated if a business or service offers, or even promises, to complete a task but fails to do so. Staff should not make undertakings which cannot be met, such as securing a hotel room when the property is fully booked. It reassures customers if the member of staff provides his name, verbally or through wearing a name tag. This helps confirm to both staff and customer that there is accountability if a promise or undertaking is not met. The philosophical principle is that the customer should not feel that she is dealing with a nameless, faceless corporate entity, where nobody can be held to account for failings.

Responsiveness to Problems

Customer service begins with providing a positive experience, but its philosophy must incorporate willingness to respond to negative situations. There are two basic elements to the response. The first acknowledges the problem and-where appropriate-makes apology for it. The second seeks to correct the problem. Good customer service takes ownership of complaints and problems. There may be a philosophical difference on the extent of recompense which should be offered. It may be sufficient to replace or repair damaged items, by replacing badly cooked food or by refunding inappropriate charges. A more generous philosophy would make extra recompense, by offering some additional benefit or service in acknowledgment of the inconvenience or distress caused.

General Helpfulness

Many customer service philosophies go beyond the provision of a positive experience within the terms of the goods or services purchased by the customer, proposing that customers should be provided with additional, wide-ranging assistance. Staff assisting a visiting customer with a purchase might also make recommendations on request about local amenities, or offer to assist the customer in ways not related to the purchase. If unable to assist, staff members may direct the customer to other sources of help, including providing telephone numbers or web addresses. Individual businesses will vary as to the extent of such helpfulness they wish their staff to provide.

Training and Monitoring

The context for an effective customer service philosophy is staff training. In addition to training staff in the provision of the goods and services expected by customers or guests, staff members must demonstrate courtesy, sincerity and attentiveness, especially in listening to and answering individual customers rather than giving generalized responses. A sophisticated approach to customer service also requires monitoring outcome. Simple surveys are one way of assessing customer satisfaction; another is measuring the extent of repeat business.

Section Ⅲ: Passage
Interpret the following passage into English.

客服在美发沙龙里的重要性

"下一个"是武装部队理发站里最常听到的一个词儿。虽然数量高于质量在这里完全行得通，但是，采取这种态度就一定会失去客户，并最终葬送自己的职业生涯。美发沙龙是一个行业，它跟所有行业一样，出色的顾客服务能稳定客户群体，确保业务经久不衰。

意义

客户没了，美发沙龙就没了。良好的客户服务是确保客户光顾的唯一方法。你必须营造一个轻松愉快的氛围，让顾客有一种宾至如归的感觉。此外，客户必须觉得你是一个可以信赖的朋友。再者，口碑传千里，口碑可以对你的沙龙产生正面或负面的影响。

益处

良好的客户服务有两大益处：巩固老客户，开拓新业务。一旦客户认为你是一个可以信赖的朋友，就会回来，即便她只需要稍微修剪一下头发。作为一种营销手段，给客户一个冰箱贴，上面写着你或你的沙龙的名字和电话号码。当客户的朋友问她是否知道哪里有一个好的美发沙龙时，你的冰箱贴就会摆在她的面前，你的新业务就来了。

对个人的忠诚

据纽约城市大学的研究，沙龙客户是与美发师而不是与沙龙建立忠诚。忠诚的客户点名要你为她服务，这对你来说无疑是一个十分有利的强大工具。建立一个忠诚的客户群，可以确保你的收益。如果你是一个独立的承包商，租了这间沙龙，那你一定会有回头客。总有一天，你会开一个属于自己的美发店。

时间上的考虑

建立一个忠诚的客户群不能一蹴而就。坚实的基础是靠时间打下的，是靠对客户的维护打下的。在这种情况下，优质客户服务的重要性就显现出来了。渐渐地，一个忠诚的客户群就建立起来了。

误解

优质客户服务并不意味着成为客户的奴隶，或者成为唯唯诺诺的人。如果客户提出要某个发型，而这个发型与她的脸型不般配，如果你照办了，结果一定很可怕。客户不会责怪自己，反而会责备你。要避免这种情况的发生，就需要机智，需要诚实。"顾客永远是对的"那句古训可能并不适用于美发沙龙。

Section Ⅰ：Dialog

店员：小姐，上午好。今天有什么能为您服务的吗？

客人：I'd like to have my hair done. But how come there are so many people here today?

店员：您看，中秋节就要到了，马上要有个小长假。节日前，人们都喜欢做头发。

客人：That makes sense. How long do I have to wait?

店员：大约半小时吧。

客人：Oh no.

店员：嗯，小姐，如果您不赶时间的话，我建议您在那边找个地方坐下，看看这本时尚杂志上最新流行的发型。说不定您也想来个变化呢。

客人：I think you are right. Thank you.

店员：您看，这有各种各样的发型——剪短发、后掠式、盘花式、齐肩式，还可以把头发挽成发髻。好好看看，待会儿我帮您选一款，一款既符合您肤色、又适合您脸型的。

客人：So many choices. That's very nice of you.

店员：慢慢看，小姐。我先照顾我的客人了。

客人：Go ahead then.

(25分钟后)

店员：不好意思，小姐，让您久等了。您选好了吗？

客人：Not really. What do you suggest?

店员：看您的肤色和五官，我想长发比较适合您。

客人：You mean shoulder-length hair style?

店员：是的，小姐。您觉得呢？

客人：I agree. You are, after all, the hairologist. I trust your eyes.

店员：很好。您还要烫一下，是吧？

客人：Yes.

店员：大花，中花，还是自然卷？

客人：I'd like to have it natural curly.

店员：好的。小姐，您以前染过发吗？

客人：Yes.

店员：今天也染吗，小姐？

客人：Yes. Could you make me a blond? You know, I'm tired of being the same color.

店员：金发？我觉得金发和您的肤色不相配。红色怎么样？今年流行红色。

客人：I don't think I'll follow the crowd this time.

店员：所以，您喜欢标新立异。很好啊。年轻就要与众不同。

客人：Naturally.

店员：好了，小姐，我的助手现在要给您洗头了。请跟他去吧。

客人：Thank you.

Section Ⅱ：Passage

客服理念

世界上没有一个统一的适用于所有产业和服务行业的客户服务理念，相反，却存在着各种各样的实践。这些实践有一个统一的信念，即客户的满意度有助于行业实现既定的目标。然而，常见的做法为客户服务提供了一些基本的准则。具体细节可能存在很大区别。例如，与远程客户打交道的金融服务公司和面对面接待客人的酒店或餐馆之间就是如此。大的公司有专门的服务团队，致力于解决这个问题。

可访问性

客户服务的哲学基础是可访问性。当面也好，通过电话或电子邮件也罢，客户需要帮助时，必须能够接触到员工，并确保得到及时回应。如果员工无法立即协助客户，无论是因为前台那里正排着长龙，还是因为有很多电话等着接听，一定要让等待的客人知道，你意识到了他的存在。如果很多人在等候电话，如果能用准确的录音信息通知对方，那么，等待就会变得不那么难受了。同样，如果查询或投诉不能得到马上处理，应该立即通知对方你已经收到了这些问题。

问责制

如果某个企业或服务机构主动提出，甚至承诺，要完成一项任务，而最终却未能兑现诺言，那么，客户会变得十分不悦。员工不应该承诺不能兑现的事情。例如，在酒店客满的情况下，不要承诺为客人订房。员工通过口头或佩戴胸牌的方式提供自己的名字，会让客户感到放心。这会让员工和客户都很清楚，一旦承诺未能兑现，有人要出来承担责任。这个哲学原则是，客户不应该觉得他面对的是一个不知其名、身份不明的企业，一个没有人会为失职承担责任的企业。

对问题的响应

客户服务始于为客户提供一个积极的体验，但这一理念当中必须包含愿意回应负面情况。回应包括两个基本元素。第一，承认问题的存在，并且在合适的情况下，予以道歉。第二，设法纠正错误。良好的客户服务包括客户的投诉权和行业解决问题的权利。在补偿问题上，可能存在理念上的差异。一种理念认为，物品受损了，换一换就成了。例如，饭菜烧坏了，换一盘；费用收多了，退回去。另一种理念则比较慷慨，就是提供额外的补偿。具体来说，是为引起的不便或造成的痛苦给客户提供一些额外的优惠或服务。

多方面帮助

许多客户服务理念远远超越了初衷，即为客户在购买商品或服务方面提供一个积极的体验，建议为客户提供额外的、广泛的援助。员工要帮助前来消费的客户，同时，还要根据客户要求，为他们提供当地福利设施方面的信息，或提供与消费无关的帮助。如果无法提供帮助，员工应该向客户推荐其他可以获得帮助的途径，包括提供电话号码或网址等。而个体商户，在为客人提供何种帮助这个问题上，各有不同。

培训和检测

有效的客户服务理念的前提是员工培训。员工除了接受培训，为客人提供所期望的产品和服务以外，还要彬彬有礼，专心致志，以诚待人，尤其是要认真倾听客人的问题，耐心回答客人的问题，而不是泛泛地一说了事。成熟的客户服务方式也需要检测。简单的调查是评估客户满意度的一种方式；客户回头率则是评估的另外一种方式。

Section Ⅲ：Passage

Importance of Customer Service in a Hair Salon

"Next" is a word most often heard at an armed forces hair cutting station. While quantity above quality may work at the station, assuming this attitude is a surefire way to lose customers and eventually lose your career. A hair salon is a business, and, like all businesses, great customer service assures repeat customers, keeping the business alive.

Significance

A hair salon will die without customers. The only way to assure that customers come in is with great customer service. You must convey an affable atmosphere and make the customer feel at home. Furthermore, the customer has to feel that you are a trusted friend. Word of mouth also travels far, with either positive or negative implications for your salon.

Benefits

Two chief benefits result from great customer service: repeat business and new business. When a customer feels that you are a trusted friend, she will come back, even if she just needs a slight trim. As a marketing tool, give the customer a refrigerator magnet with your (or your salon's) name and phone number on it. When a customer's friend asks if she knows a good salon, your magnet is right there in front of her, and you are assured new business.

Personal Loyalty

According to the City University of New York, salon customers establish loyalty to the hairdresser, not to the salon. Loyal customers will ask for you by name. This is undoubtedly a powerful tool to your advantage. By building a loyal customer base, you are assured earnings. If you are an independent contractor renting the salon space, you can assure yourself repeat business. Some day, you may even open up your own shop.

Time Considerations

Building up a loyal customer base does not happen overnight. A solid base is built up over time, servicing many customers. In this case, the importance of good customer service becomes apparent. Little by little, a loyal customer base will be built up.

Misconceptions

Great customer service does not mean becoming a slave to the customer, or becoming a yes-man. If the customer suggests a hair style that will clash with her facial features, and you give it to her, the results will look terrible. The customer will not blame herself; she will blame you. To avoid this, you need to use tact and be honest. The old adage "the customer is always right" may not be applicable in a hair salon.

第10单元
投诉处理

Handling Complaints

课文 1　　Text A

Section Ⅰ: Dialog
Interpret the following dialog alternatively into English and Chinese.

大堂副理：Hello. This is David Yang, Assistant Manager of the Hotel. Can I help you, ma'am?

客户：嗯。我叫珍妮·泰勒。我在 8567 房间。昨天，我把一件衬衣和两条裙子拿去洗了。可是，今天早上拿回来时，发现衬衣上两粒扣子没了，而且，一条裙子上还有一块油渍。

大堂副理：I'm terribly sorry to hear that, ma'am. Did you call the Housekeeping Department?

客户：打了，刚打。可是，没有人接电话。

大堂副理：This is quite unusual. Probably they had an emergency to attend to. Anyway I will look into the matter. By the way, are you sure the buttons were still there when your laundry bag was collected, ma'am?

客户：你什么意思？你觉得我在撒谎？

大堂副理：No, no, no, ma'am. No hard feelings. I assure you that that was certainly not my intention. I was just checking. I mean the buttons could have fallen off the shirt somewhere in your room. Have you looked in your room, ma'am?

客户：找了，可是哪儿也找不到。也许你觉得我这个人不好说话，拿两粒扣子太当回事了。

大堂副理：No, not at all, ma'am. Don't get offended.

客户：你知道吗？那件衬衣恰巧是我们结婚 25 周年时我丈夫送给我的礼物。

大堂副理：I see. That's a memorable gift.

客户：现在，你该明白我刚才激动的原因了吧？

大堂副理：Yes, I do, ma'am.

客户：所以，你们打算怎么处理，先生？

大堂副理：I'll call the Housekeeping Department right away.

客户：请吧。

大堂副理：Sorry, the line is busy. Hold on a second, ma'am. I'll try again.

客户：好的。我等着。

大堂副理：Sorry, still busy. Well, ma'am, how do you want this handled?

客户：你们要么派人给我找到扣子，把裙子上的油渍去掉，要么赔偿我的损失。

大堂副理：That's reasonable enough. If someone finds your buttons, I will send her right up to you. And she will sew them on your shirt. I will also ask the Housekeeping Department to have the oil stain treated.

客户：好的。可是，要是事与愿违呢？

大堂副理：I don't want to see things happen that way. But, if they do, we'll compensate for your losses according to the rules and regulations of the hotel. Will that be OK with you, ma'am?

客户：可以。咱们还是往好处想吧。

大堂副理：You are a very understanding lady. You may get off the phone now, ma'am. Thanks a lot.

Section Ⅱ：Passage
Interpret the following passage into Chinese.

Guest Complaint Guidelines of Westin

If you observe, encounter or have a problem brought to your attention, make every attempt to resolve the matter. It is very important that you listen and try to resolve all problems to ensure guest satisfaction. All complaints must be relayed to a manager or supervisor before the guest leaves the premises. Telephone calls from emotional or anxious guests should be treated in the same concerned, friendly manner as a "typical" call. You need to maintain control of the conversation and find a satisfactory resolution to the guests' needs in an efficient manner.

Listen with concern and do not interrupt the guest.

Isolate the guest so that other guests do not hear the discussion.

Remain calm and speak softly—do not argue or give excuses to the guest; remain impartial and flexible.

Make every effort to discover the cause of the problem.

Apologize for the problem regardless of who is right or wrong.

Empathize with the guest; show that you understand how he/she is feeling and that you are concerned about the situation.

Do not take complaints personally!

Use the guest's name frequently and take the complaint seriously no matter how minor it may seem.

Summarize your understanding of the complaint in your own words back to the guest.

Take notes while the guest is informing you of the problem.

If the complaint is in reference to a hotel policy:

Look for alternative solutions, such as resolving the guest's complaint another way.

If no alternatives are available, clearly explain to the guest why the policy exists without becoming defensive.

Remedy the situation and ask the guest "What would you like us to do?" Usually the guest will ask for less than what we would be prepared to give. Most guests who complain want an understanding of the problem so that it can be resolved.

Thank the guest for bringing the problem/situation to our attention and allowing us the opportunity to rectify the problem.

Do exactly what you promised the guest.

Accept responsibility for the resolving of the situation. Do not refer the guest to someone else.

Never attempt to lay the blame on other departments or associates.

Follow up with the guest to make certain the solution was satisfactory.

Record all pertinent information in the appropriate logbook, including any guest history information.

Review the problem with your manager to determine how we can avoid similar situations in the future.

Section Ⅲ: Passage
Interpret the following passage into English.

如何处理客户投诉

所有以顾客为导向的企业都必须准备处理客户投诉。客户是否想退回有缺陷的产品，是否愿意接受差劲的服务，取决于企业如何处理投诉，如何为客户提供帮助。培训客服代表以恭敬的态度、专业的方式处理投诉，能提高公司的形象，创建一个强大的客户群。以下几点是经理人应该特别注意的。

首先，设法弄清问题。

培训员工弄清客户的问题，并重申客户的问题，这会使客户产生一种有人愿意倾听、有人理解自己的感觉。要耐心倾听客户的投诉，用自己的话重复一遍。可以这样开始："所以，您的意思是……"或者"按照我对这个问题的理解，您的意思是……"，以此来重申客户的诉求。永远不要与客户争辩，否则，客户会更加愤怒，并开始防备你。与此同时，不是什么事情都得向客户道歉，没有义务去接受客户的侮辱谩骂。只求用公平、公正的方式去倾听，并弄清客户投诉的问题所在。

第二，尽量提供帮助。

在弄清客户的投诉后，要承认问题的存在，并提供帮助。可以这样说："看来，您对我们的服务不太满意。我能做些什么来解决这个问题吗？"让客户自己说出他认为最好的解决办法。告诉客户可以退货，可以退款，也可以免费提供维修服务。考虑向客户做出一个额外的让步。比如，客户将来购物时，可以打个折扣。这样，可以改善公司与顾客之间的关系，增加顾客的回头率。

第三，学会表示感谢。

在解决了客户的投诉之后，感谢他的反馈意见。即便客户向公司表达的是负面情绪，也要感谢他，这可以证明公司是以恭敬的态度、专业的方式对待所有客户。进一步询问客户，对公司的业务和客服是否还有别的意见。这表明公司愿意提高服务水平，满足顾客的需求。

第四，知道如何处理不良行为。

客服代表不需要忍受客户的辱骂与伤害。如果客户进行口头谩骂或人身攻击，要用专业的方式去处理这种不良行为。要用坚定的语气告诉他："如果您继续使用这样的言语，我将不得不让您离开。"或者，使用类似的言语，表达你不能接受客户这种令人发指的行为。如果客户继续这种不当行为，要立即联系经理。如果客户威胁你的人身安全，那么，请马上报警。

Section Ⅰ：Dialog

大堂副理：您好，我是大堂副理杨大卫。有什么能为您效劳的吗，夫人？

客户： Yes. This is Jane Tayor in Room 8567. I had a shirt and two skirts laundered yesterday. But when I got them back this morning, I found that there were two buttons missing from the shirt, and there was an oil stain on one of the skirts.

大堂副理：听到这个消息，我很抱歉，夫人。您给客房部打电话了吗？

客户：Yes, I did a while ago. But nobody answered the phone.

大堂副理：这极不正常。也许他们有急事要处理。不管怎么说，我都要调查此事。对了，您确定服务员拿衣服袋时扣子还在吗，夫人？

客户：What are you driving at? You think I'm a liar?

大堂副理：不不不，夫人。别见怪。我保证不是那个意思。我就是问问。我的意思是说，扣子可能脱落在您屋子的什么地方。您在屋子里找了吗，夫人？

客户：Yes, I have. But they are nowhere to be found. Maybe you think that I'm a difficult person, and that I take two buttons too seriously.

大堂副理：没有，根本没有，夫人。千万别生气。

客户：You know what? That shirt happens to be a gift from my husband on our 25th wedding anniversary.

大堂副理：明白了。那是个很有纪念意义的礼物。

客户：Now you understand why I was a little excited just now, don't you?

大堂副理：是的，我知道，夫人。

客户：So what are you going to do about it, sir?

大堂副理：我马上给客房部打电话。

客户：Go ahead then.

大堂副理：不好意思，占线。请稍等，夫人。我再打。

客户：OK. I'm right here, waiting.

大堂副理：对不起，还是占线。嗯，夫人，您希望怎么处理？

客户：You either ask someone to find the buttons for me, and get the stain out of my skirt or compensate for my losses.

大堂副理：合情合理。如果有人找到了您的扣子，我会马上派她过去，给您缝上。我还会让客房部把油渍处理了。

客户：That's good. But what if things go the other way?

大堂副理：我不希望看到那样的情况发现。不过，万一如此，我们会根据酒店规定给您赔偿。这样可以吗，夫人？

客户：Yes. Let's hope for the best.

大堂副理：您真的很通情达理。您现在可以挂电话了，夫人。多谢。

Section II : Passage

威斯汀投诉处理指南

如果你发现了问题，遇到了问题，如果有人把问题交给了你，那就想方设法去解决吧。重要的是，你要认真倾听，试图解决所有问题，确保客户得到满意的答复。所有投诉都必须在客户离开之前转达给经理或主管。如果打进电话的客户情绪激动或焦躁不安，应该和处理普通电话一样，以关心友好地态度进行处理。你要控制对话的节奏，以有效的方式找到满足客户需求的途径。

认真倾听，不要打断客户。

把客户和其他客人隔开，这样，别人就听不到你们之间的谈话了。

保持冷静，轻声说话；不要争论，不要找借口；做到公正、灵活。

千方百计发现问题的根源。

出现问题，就要道歉，无论谁对谁错。

对客人表现出同情的态度；向客人表明，你理解他们的感受，对眼前的问题十分关心。

不要把投诉看成是针对你个人的行为！

经常称呼客户的名字，认真对待投诉，不管它看起来是多么无关紧要。

用自己的话跟客户说明你对投诉的理解。

客人投诉时，要亲笔记下来。

如果投诉针对的是酒店的政策，那么，要去寻找替代方案，如采用另一种方式解决客户的投诉。

如果没有现成的替代方案，要明确地向客户解释为什么会有这样的政策，不要让人觉得你是在替酒店辩护。

采取补救措施，问问客户："您希望我们怎么办？"通常，客户开出的价码要低于我们的预期。大多数投诉的客户都希望得到我们的理解，这样，问题就好解决了。

感谢客户让我们注意到问题的存在，让我们有机会来纠正这个问题。

答应客户的，就一定要做到。

要负起责任，主动解决问题。不要把客户推给别人。

永远不要把责任推给其他部门或别的同事。

做好后续工作，确保客户对解决方法感到满意。

做好相关记录，包括客户的历史信息。

与经理一起把问题重新梳理一遍，看看如何避免今后出现类似的情况。

Section Ⅲ : Passage

How to Deal with Customer Complaints?

All customer-oriented businesses must be prepared to deal with customer complaints. Whether a customer wants to return a defective item or receives poor service, it is up to the business to address complaints and offer help. Training customer service representatives to deal with complaints in a respectful, professional manner improves the company's image and creates a strong customer base. Here are a few points you should pay special attention to as a manager.

First, try to identify the problem.

Teach employees to identify and restate a customer's problem. This makes the customer feel as though he is being heard and understood. Listen patiently to a customer's complaints and restate it in your own words. Begin with a phrase such as "So what you are saying is that …" or "As I understand the problem, you feel that…" to reframe the customer's complaint. Never argue with the customer, which can cause him to become defensive and angrier. At the same time, do not feel obligated to apologize or take abuse from a customer. Simply listen and identify the customer's complaint in a fair, unbiased way.

Second, try to offer help.

After identifying the customer's complaint, acknowledge the problem and offer to help. Say "It seems like you are unhappy with the service you received. What can I do to address this problem?" Allow the customer to state what he thinks is the best solution to the problem. Offer to allow the customer to return an item, receive money back or receive free repair services. Consider offering an additional concession to the customer, such as a discount on future merchandise. This improves your company's relationship with the customer and increases the odds that he will return.

Third, learn to express thanks.

After resolving a customer's complaint, thank him for his feedback. By thanking a customer even when he expresses negative feelings toward your company, you demonstrate that your company treats all customers respectfully and professionally. Ask the customer if he has further feedback on your company's business practices and customer service. This demonstrates a willingness to improve services to meet customer needs.

Fourth, know how to deal with poor behavior.

A customer service representative does not need to put up with abuse from a customer. If a customer becomes verbally abusive or personally threatening, professionally address the poor behavior. Firmly state "I will have to ask you to leave if you continue to use that language" or a similar phrase expressing your intolerance for unacceptable customer behavior. If the customer continues to behave inappropriately, contact your manager immediately. Call the police if a customer threatens your physical safety.

课文 2　Text B

Section Ⅰ: Dialog
Interpret the following dialog alternatively into English and Chinese.

客户: Hello. This is Susan O'neil. May I speak to the Assistant Manager, please?

大堂副理：我就是。能为您效劳吗，夫人？
客户：Yes, Mr. ... ?
大堂副理：免贵姓房。
客户：Mr. Fang, I've just checked in and have found some problems.
大堂副理：什么问题？
客户：You see, the whole room is in a total mess. I'm not happy about it.
大堂副理：真不知道怎么会发生这样的事情，夫人。
客户：The bed sheets are dirty, and the pillows are on the floor. The ashtray on the tea table is filled with cigarette butts. There are two empty beer cans on the table below the mirror. And there is also garbage in the waster paper basket.
大堂副理：非常抱歉，夫人。请告诉我您的房间号码。
客户：8216
大堂副理：您是说走廊尽头那个房间？
客户：Exactly.
大堂副理：明白了。您知道吗，夫人，您前面的客户很晚才退房，而您又要马上入住，所以，服务员来不及整理。另外，我们今天人手不够。
客户：You see, the hand towels and bath towels are all in the filthy tub. I can't stay in such a room. So can you change the room for me now?
大堂副理：对不起，夫人，现在没有房间。有一个20多人的旅游团明天上午离店。到那个那时候，您就可以随意挑选了，夫人。
客户：What shall I do now?
大堂副理：我现在就派服务员前去打扫，您看行吗？
客户：OK. But where am I supposed to stay while she's doing her job?
大堂副理：我会派一个行李员过去，他会照看您的行李，送您去楼层贵宾室。您看这样成吗，夫人？
客户：That's good.
大堂副理：带来不便，十分抱歉，夫人。感谢您的理解与合作。
客户：I can't lay the blame entirely on you. I'm to blame as well. I was a bit impatient.
大堂副理：您真大度。您是十足的大家闺秀！
客户：I think my face is red, Mr. Fang?
大堂副理：我不是说着玩儿的，奥尼尔夫人。相信您下次再来时，一切都会让您称心如意的。
客户：I believe you.
大堂副理：跟您说个事，奥尼尔夫人，您整个入住期间的房费将打9.5折。
客户：Oh, thank you. I will certainly come again. I promise I will.
大堂副理：我们会竭诚为您服务，夫人。祝您在此度过入住愉快。
客户：Thanks.

Section II: Passage
Interpret the following passage into Chinese.

Customer Relationship Management Ideas for the 21st Century

Customer relationship management deals with tools, methods and strategies to manage customer relationships in an organized and effective way. According to a report, the cost of acquiring a new customer is six to seven times more than keeping an existing customer. In addition, the report also says that over a five year period there is an attrition rate of one half of a company's customers.

These two statistics make a compelling case for employing 21st Century customer relationship management ideas to reduce costs and retain customers. There are several customer relationship management strategies that can have a significant impact.

Customization

According to the website Hotel Interactive, the next generation of customer relationship management provides the ability to create customized services and products to meet the needs of individual consumers. In the hotel business, prices can be set based on customer loyalty. This concept can be applied to most industries. For example, a clothing retailer could send customized mailings to customers based on the type of clothing they've bought in the past. When new selections arrive in a store, mail could be sent suggesting a clothing ensemble.

Social Media

According to the website Enterprise Systems, social media is impacting customer relationship management because consumers can quickly spread their positive and negative views of a company through social media.

Companies must now be even more focused on delivering optimum customer service, constantly assessing and correcting any incorrect negative information in the marketplace, and become proactively involved in social media marketing as part of the overall customer relationship management strategies.

Social media can also be used as a valuable and instantaneous feedback medium for a company to connect to its customers.

Technology

According to the Journal of Management and Organization referring to the future of relationship marketing, improvements in customer data collection and analysis provide for the opportunity to tailor messages to individual targeted consumers. One example is Google's display of its advertising messages based on the content of an individual's email address. In terms of customer habits and buying patterns, Internet technology is able to provide volumes of data by user type about their use of the Internet.

This type of data gathering will continue to be questioned, putting at odds the marketer's hunger for data and the consumer's interest in privacy.

Internet

According to Information Week, the Internet has allowed companies to more easily adapt to customer needs. For example, when purchasing on the Internet, a customer can choose shipping method, and for some online retailers, customize what they are ordering. One example of customized ordering is Cafe Press, a site selling clothing and premium type items, which allows you to place messages you specify on these items.

Section Ⅲ: Passage
Interpret the following passage into English.

客户投诉处理指南

在经常与公众打交道的几乎任何公司，客户投诉都是不可避免的。无论是对产品的投诉，还是对服务的投诉，客户的不满源于其期望值与实际之间的差异。成功的企业会建立一个客户投诉流程，有助于留住客户，避免负面宣传，帮助改进公司流程，提高客服水平。尽管心中不满的客户难以应对，但是，正确的态度和完善的公司政策可以把负面的情况变成积极的结果。

第一，建立一个简单的客户投诉反馈机制。允许客户通过信函、电子邮件、传真和电话与公司联系。联系的方式越简单，了解客户合理投诉的可能性就越大，失去客户的可能性就越小。

第二，建立一个常规上报流程。这个流程应该涵盖包括紧急情况在内的所有类型的客户投诉，并提供指导方针和联系方式。把上述信息提供给所有可能与客户打交道的员工，根据级别明确分工。例如，客服人员应当把问题汇报给经理，而不是信息技术部门。

第三，设计一个跟踪机制。成功处理客户投诉，要求对投诉进行有效的指导和管理。跟踪系统不仅可以通过有效的方式实时处理投诉，还为长期分析和复盘提供了有用的数据。

第四，要建立"终止"程序。有些客户可能非常不可理喻，仅仅为了一己私利经常投诉。建立该程序，让员工知道何时终止事态升级，何时终止为难缠的客户提供额外的帮助。例如，对那些想越过主管经理升级投诉的胡搅蛮缠的客户，要求他们以书面的方式提出自己的请求。这种机制有助于关注合理的投诉，避免无意义的投诉。

第五，监控客户投诉的趋势或模式。如果很多客户都进行类似的投诉，那么，这就是一种先兆，说明企业内部出现了大问题，需要认真面对了。处理投诉最好的方法就是阻止投诉的发生。

第六，培训各级员工，掌握适当处理客户投诉的方法。培训应赋予员工快速解决问题的权利，还应提供有效的会话训练，帮助员工安抚愤怒的客户。

参考答案

Section Ⅰ：Dialog

客户：你好。我是苏珊·奥尼尔。我找大堂副理。

大堂副理：This is he. Can I be of any assistance, ma'am?

客户：先生，请问贵姓？

大堂副理：Fang.

客户：房先生，我刚刚入住，发现了一些问题。

大堂副理：What are they?

客户：你看，整个房间一团乱麻。我很不满意。

大堂副理：I don't know how that could have happened, ma'am.

客户：床单是脏的，枕头都在地板上；茶几上的烟灰缸满满的，都是烟蒂；镜子下面的桌子上有两个空啤酒罐；废纸篓里还有垃圾。

大堂副理：I'm awfully sorry, ma'am. What is the number of your room, please?

客户：8216。

大堂副理：You mean the one at the end of the corridor?

客户：是的。

大堂副理：I see. You know something, ma'am? The guest before you checked out late, and you demanded immediate access to your room. So the chambermaid didn't have time to make it up. Besides, we are short of hands today.

客户：你看，毛巾、浴巾都在脏兮兮的浴缸里。我不能住在这样的房间里，所以，你可以马上给我换一个房间吗？

大堂副理：I'm sorry, ma'am. We don't have any rooms available now. A tourist group of over 20 people will leave tomorrow morning. Then you can choose whichever room you like, ma'am.

客户：那我现在怎么办？

大堂副理：Do you think it good if I send a chambermaid to make up your bed immediately?

客户：行。可是，服务员收拾房间时，我待在哪里？

大堂副理：I'll send a porter to you right now. He'll take care of your luggage, and take you to the VIP room on your floor. Is that OK, ma'am?

客户：那成。

大堂副理：I do apologize for the inconvenience caused, ma'am. Thank you for your understanding and cooperation.

客户：也不能全怪你，也怪我太急。

大堂副理：You are very generous. You are every inch a lady.

客户：我的脸红了吧，房先生？

大堂副理：I mean it, Mrs. O'neil. I'm sure everything will be right again next time you come.

客户：我相信你。

大堂副理：Let me tell you what, Mrs. O'neil. You'll get a 5% discount of your room rate during your entire stay in our hotel.

客户： 噢，谢谢。我一定会再来的。一定。

大堂副理：We'll try our best to accommodate you, ma'am. Have a pleasant stay here.

客户：谢谢。

Section Ⅱ：Passage

21世纪客户关系管理理念

客户关系管理涉及有序、有效管理客户关系所需要的工具、方法和策略。根据一份报告的研究，开发一个新客户所需的成本是保持现有客户的6至7倍。此外，报告还说，企业每五年就会流失一半客户。

这两个统计数据迫使人们利用21世纪客户关系管理理念来降低成本和保留客户。下面几个客户关系管理策略能够产生重大的影响。

量身定制

根据"酒店互动"网站的信息，下一代客户关系管理能够推出量身定制的服务和产品，来满足个人消费者的需求。在酒店业，价格可以根据客户的忠诚度来定。这一概念可以应用于大多数行业。例如，服装零售商可以根据客户以往购买服装的类型发送专门定制的邮件。当新款上市时，可以给客户发送邮件，推荐套装。

社交媒体

根据"企业系统"网站的内容,社交媒体正影响着客户关系管理,因为消费者可以通过社交媒体迅速传播他们对企业的正面看法和负面看法。

如今,企业必须更加专注于提供最优质的客户服务,不断评估和修正自己在市场上的任何负面形象,积极参与社交媒体营销,将其视为客户关系管理策略的一个有机组成部分。

此外,还可以把社交媒体当成企业联系客户的重要的瞬时反馈手段。

技术

根据关系营销未来杂志《管理和组织》上的文章,客户数据收集和分析方面的改进使企业有机会为目标客户提供量身定制的信息。例如,谷歌根据个人电子邮件地址方面的信息发送相应的广告。说到客户习惯和购买模式,互联网技术能够根据用户类型,提供大量的网络使用情况信息。

这种类型的数据收集将继续受到质疑,因为它将营销人员对信息的渴望和消费者对隐私的关注对立起来。

互联网

根据《信息周刊》的消息,互联网能使企业更加容易地适应顾客的需求。例如,网上购物时,客户可以选择运输方法。对某些网络零售商来说,还可以为客户量身打造订单。比如,一个名叫"咖啡影印"的出售服装和溢价商品的网站,可以在出售的商品上印上客户指定的信息。

Section Ⅲ: Passage

Customer Complaint Techniques

Customer complaints are inevitable in almost any company that interacts with the public on a regular basis. From product complaints to service-related complaints, customers like to express their frustration based on a discrepancy between their expectations and their actual experience. Successful companies establish a customer complaint process that helps retain the customer, prevents negative publicity and helps improve company processes and customer service. While unhappy customers can be challenging to manage, the right attitude and company policies can turn a negative situation into a positive outcome.

First, create a simple feedback mechanism for customers to lodge complaints. Allow customers to contact your company through mail, email, fax and by phone. The easier the contact process, the more likely you will know about valid complaints and the less likely you are to lose customers.

Second, establish a routine escalation process. This process should encompass all types of customer complaints, including emergency situations, with guidelines and contact information. Provide this information to all employees who may encounter customers, customized according to their rank. For example, a customer service agent should direct escalations to their manager rather than the information technology department.

Third, devise a tracking mechanism. Successful management of customer complaints requires directing and managing complaints effectively. A tracking system not only provides a real-time way of processing complaints in an efficient manner, it also provides helpful data for longer-term analysis and review.

Fourth, put stop procedures in place. Some customers may be impossible to please and may routinely lodge complaints merely for their benefit. Establish procedures for when to stop escalations and stop providing out-of-bounds assistance to unreasonable customers. For example, require unreasonable customers who want to escalate complaints beyond the immediate manager to provide their request in writing. This provides a mechanism for a true customer concern, but discourages frivolous complaints.

Fifth, monitor customer complaints for trends or patterns. Similar complaints from multiple customers can be an early indicator of a wider business problem that you need to address. The best process for customer complaints is to prevent them from occurring.

Sixth, train all levels of employees on proper customer complaint management. This training should empower employees to resolve issues quickly and needs to provide helpful dialogue training that can help employees calm irate customers.

附录

口译对策

Coping Tactics

一、顺译方法

所谓顺译法，顾名思义，就是按原句的顺序翻译。这与字对字的死译完全不同，其翻译单位是"意群"。顺译不仅是一种方法，更是一种原则，这是由口译的特点所决定的。口译的特点是即时性，口译人员没有充足的时间推敲琢磨。因此，为了提高效率，确保译文的口语化，减轻听众的负担，唯一的办法就是顺句驱动。

英汉两种语言在词序、语序上存在着较大的差异，因此，译员要根据意群及时"断句"。这一点与古代的"句读"颇有异曲同工之妙。实践中，可以根据自身的条件一个意群一个意群地翻译，也可以一两个意群连在一起翻译。一句话分成若干意群，然后通过句法手段、修辞手段连成一体，听上去自然地道。这就要求译者放弃以往笔译中颠倒语序重新组句的习惯，进行逆向思维。以下为例句。

(1) China is a developing country // with a population of 1.3 billion, // of whom 300 million are children under the age of 16, // making up about one fifth of the total number of children in the world.

中国是发展中国家，人口13亿，其中约3亿为16岁以下的儿童，约占世界儿童总数的1/5。

(2) We need to prepare for the negotiations now, // by taking a comprehensive approach // and injecting a sense of urgency, //if we are to bring them to a successful and early conclusion.

我们现在就需要为谈判作准备，要有全局观念，要有紧迫感，只有这样，才能尽快达成一致。

(3) China's membership of the WTO // is a good example // of how integrating it more fully into the international system // works to all of our advantage.

中国入世充分表明，中国全面融入国际社会对大家都有好处。

(4) The home and yard environment will also be improved // with the development of genetically-engineered lawns // that require fewer or no chemical treatments.

室内环境和庭院环境也将得到改善，这都得益于基因草坪的问世，这种草坪几乎不需要化学除草。

(5) In this most beautiful autumn season, // we welcome in Beijing the opening of the Fourth World Conference on Women, // the largest and one of the most important international meetings of its kind in world history.

在这个美丽的金秋时节，我们在北京迎来了第四届世界妇女大会的召开。这是世界史上规模最大、最为重要的国际会议之一。

(6) As Asia's world city, // Hong Kong is a widely acclaimed tourist desti-

nation // known for its international outlook, sophistication and diversity.

作为亚洲的一座世界级城市,香港是备受欢迎的旅游目的地,以其国际面貌和丰富多彩而闻名遐迩。

(7) 首先,请允许我//代表中国贸易代表团,并且以我个人名义,//对大家的盛情邀请和热情接待表示衷心的感谢,//对长期以来为促进中南经贸关系发展、增进中南人民友谊做出积极贡献的各界人士表示诚挚的敬意。

First of all, please allow me to express, on behalf of the Chinese trade delegation, and also in my own name, our profound gratitude for your kind invitation and gracious hospitality, and to send our greatest respects to all those who have made great contributions to the promotion of the development of China-South Africa trade relations and the friendship between our two peoples.

另外,还有一些常见的连词,在翻译时必须反其道而译之。如 before、after (following)、although 等应分别译成"之后""此前""不过"或者"但是"等。

(1) Work before pleasure.

这句话只能采取反译的方法,译成"工作在前,享乐在后"或者"工作第一,享乐第二"。

(2) Eat it before it gets cold.

这句话可以译成"趁热吃吧",也可以译成"吃吧,待会儿就凉了"。

(3) There are 10 minutes before we call it a day.

这句话根据不同情形可分别译成"10 分钟后下班""10 分钟后下课""10 分钟后散会"以及"10 分钟后结束"等。

(4) Look around before you come to my office.

先到处转转,然后到我办公室来。

(5) The meeting will resume at 3 p.m. after the Board of Trustees has met briefly.

会议下午 3 点继续,此前校董事会要碰个头。

(6) The Palestinians fired rockets into Israel following the Israeli bombing of West Bank and Gaza Strip.

巴勒斯坦人向以色列发射了火箭弹,此前,以色列轰炸了西岸和加沙地区。

(7) The deal will allow UN weapon inspectors' unconditional access to all suspected weapon sites. That includes 8 presidential palaces, although on those visits, diplomats will also have to be present.

该协议将允许联合国武器核查人员无条件进入所有被怀疑可能藏匿武器的地方,这包括 8 处总统官邸。不过(可是、但是、当然),对总统官邸进行核查时需要有外交官在场。

二、口译笔记

俗话说，好记性不如烂笔头。这句话在口译过程中显得尤为重要。由于口译现场时间紧，压力大，译者很难在有限的时间内记住全部信息。因此，为了保证信息的完整性和翻译的准确性，笔记便变得十分重要。

那么，笔记究竟记些什么呢？口译笔记，不同于一般速记，不求全，更不求细。一般而言，主要围绕"何人、何事、何时、何地、何由"五大方面来记录。此外，还包括数字、机构名称、技术术语等重要信息。

那么，如何做笔记呢？由于口译笔记只是补记忆之不足，且有"临时性"的特点，我们可以借助关键词、符号、图表等形式，把发言人的讲话重点、要点速记下来，以防遗漏。纸张要纵向分页，信息要阶梯式排列，这样条理清楚，重点突出。如果是站着工作，笔记本不宜过大，手掌大小最为合适。如果是坐着工作，有写字台，则大小纸张都可以，但最好不要超过 A4。另外，口译笔记宜少不宜多、宜精不宜粗。语言可以是目的语，也可以是源语，中间更是可以插入一些常见的符号或独创的符号。总之，只要能"激活"译者的记忆，什么方法都是好方法。

说到符号，常见的如下。

< 少于；不如；弱　　　　　　<< 远远少于；远不如
\> 多于；强　　　　　　　　　>> 多得多；强得多
= 等于；相同；一样　　　　　% 百分比
≈ 近似；约等于；差不多　　　X 错误；否定；不同意；禁止
√ 准确；同意；支持　　　　　≠ 不同；不等于
∶ 想　　　　　　　　　　　　" 说；宣布；陈述
? 问题；疑问　　　　　　　　☆ 重要的
& 和；与　　　　　　　　　　∥ 结束
+ 加上；优点　　　　　　　　- 减去；弱点
⊙ 国家；民族；人民　　　　　⊕ 医院
/ 与……的关系　　　　　　　∞ 总是
♀ 女　　　　　　　　　　　　♂ 男
↑ 上升；增加　　　　　　　　↓ 下降；减少
↗ 渐增；改进；发展；加速　　↘ 渐减；恶化；减速
← 来自；源自；出发　　　　　→ 导致；结果；到达

常见的字母缩写如下。

e. g. 比如；例如　　　　　　　dept 部门
pol 政治　　　　　　　　　　dem 民主
lib 自由的　　　　　　　　　info 信息
gov't 政府　　　　　　　　　intro 介绍、引入

bkgd 背景　　　　　　　　　　　bldg 大楼；建筑
cont'd 继续　　　　　　　　　　edu 教育
vs 反对　　　　　　　　　　　　ibid 同上
eco 经济

当然，每个人都可以根据自己的爱好、习惯，发明一套适合自己的速记方案。下面看几个实例。

(1) On the occasion of the Fifth International Fair for Investment and Trade, I would like to extend, on behalf of the Qingdao government, my warm welcome to our distinguished guests from all over the world.

5th int'l fair 4 invst & trad

I 4 QD gov't

wlcm 2 guests ← wrld

(2) "三农"工作进一步加强。中央财政用于"三农"的支出7253亿元，增长21.8%。大幅度提高粮食最低收购价。继续改善农村生产生活条件，农村饮水安全工程使6069万农民受益，新增510万沼气用户，新建和改造农村公路38万千米、农村电网线路26.6万千米，又有80万户农村危房得到改造，9.2万户游牧民实现了定居。

3 农 +

央财支 725.3 bln

21.8% ↑

+ + minim grain procure prix

↑ rural livin condi

H2o proj benef

60.69 mln

5.1 mln new 沼气 users

建 & 改 rd　38 万 km

pwr grid 26.6 万 km

80 万 危房 改

9.2 万户 nomads settld

(3) 青岛大学与美国全球教育联盟联合举办的高等教育国际化研讨会今天正式开幕了。首先，我谨代表青岛大学对各位来宾和与会代表表示热烈欢迎，对迪克逊博士及各位美方朋友对此次联合会议的筹办所付出的巨大努力表示衷心感谢！

qdu ＋　GEA

hi'er ed. globl

guest ＋　reps　欢

dr. Dixon ＋　友　　努力　thx

(4) It is a real pleasure to be here to open the third meeting of our forum and to be welcoming such a distinguished and influential group of people from both our countries, many of whom are now old friends. The forum aims to represent the strength of the relationship between our two countries outside the political relationship and looking round today it is clear that the relationship is very strong indeed.

@ 主 3rd　4rum
欢 2 口　有识　人 >> 老友
strength / relation
x pol
strong

三、记忆训练

研究表明，人的记忆一般分为三种：瞬时记忆、短时记忆和长时记忆。

瞬时记忆只能使语言信息保持很短的时间，大约 0.25 秒至 2 秒，此后信息便会自动消失。瞬时记忆对于同声传译至关重要。可以毫不夸张地说，没有瞬时获取信息的能力，想做口译无异于异想天开。因此，瞬时记忆是口译的前提。

短时记忆，顾名思义，持续的时间较短，但比瞬时记忆要长。短时记忆的功能是把大脑捕捉到的信息暂时保存起来。然而，由于短时记忆很短，译者必须高度集中精神，调动所有因素，积极利用这些"暂存"的信息，进行两种语言之间的转化。可见，短时记忆是口译的关键。

长时记忆是人类获取知识的重要途径。没有长时记忆，人类的信息无法传递，知识无法传承。换言之，译员平时积累的东西越多，知识面越广，工作起来越有利，因为在口译过程中，是短时记忆和长时记忆共同作用才能完成记忆工作的。所以，长时记忆是口译的基础。

既然记忆对于口译如此重要，那么，如何延长自己的短时记忆则是口译成败的关键。一般来说，主要有以下几种方法。

（一）跟读练习

口译的基础是听懂原文，也就是要抓住信息。要想听懂原文，抓住关键的信息，重要的是要熟悉各种各样的"变体"，各种各样的口音。这就要求译员一开始要进行一段时间的跟读练习。跟读的目的不是简单地模仿，而是捕捉原文的大意，并进行复述。比如：

This city of 12 million seemed to be a good place to see how a National Geographic Magazine story is put together. Istanbul, a metropolis poised on both the European and Asian continents, lies right on the fault line that could rupture anytime. This city began sometime around 657 B. C. and has reinvented itself over and over throughout the centuries.

听完这一段文字后,译员的脑子里应出现一些重要的信息点:1200 万人口、大都市、位于欧亚洲大陆之间、断裂线、公元前 657 年、今日变化等。之后,通过复述把它们连接起来,这样就达到了记忆的目的。

(二) 逻辑记忆

口译的记忆训练和考试前填鸭式的突击背诵完全不同。口译的记忆训练是建立在逻辑的基础之上的。这样的记忆是连贯的,不是杂乱无章的。在这一阶段,译员仍然需要进行复述练习,通过逻辑,把原文大意"连接起来",形成一个有意义的整体。比如:

Sports help us learn cooperation. As the saying goes, there is no "I" in teamwork.

有人将此句译成"体育让人们学会合作精神。俗话说得好,在团队里没有'大写的我'"。该译文虽然字面上完全对等,但十分晦涩难懂。不难看出,"Sports help us learn cooperation"是中心句,为后面的文字定了调子。因此,按照逻辑关系,后面的一切都是围绕集体而不是个人展开的。故这里的 I 是"自我"的意思,因为"团队精神"讲究的是合作,而不是个人英雄主义。所以,后半句应译成"俗话说得好,在团队里没有'小我'"。可见,逻辑推理在锁定意义的同时,也有助于译员的记忆。

(三) 形象记忆

形象记忆,也可以称之为记忆的视觉化,或视觉化记忆。图式理论认为,人的记忆可以以"图示"的方式呈现出来。也就是说,当译员听到一段文字之后,可以通过联想在大脑里构成一幅图画,这样能大大提高大脑的记忆功能。蓝天、大海、沙漠、草原给人们带来的是完全不同的视觉冲击。拿草原来说,它可能给人带来这样的画面或者想象:蓝蓝的天空、无垠的草地、成群的牛羊、清澈的河水、豪爽的牧民等。可见,形象记忆可在一定程度上减轻大脑的负担。

(四) 情景记忆

情景记忆是学习语言的一个很好的途径,也是提高口译记忆力的一个很好的方法。比如,如果发言人讲的是与示威游行有关的内容,译员可以根据自身的经验、常识、知识,在大脑里反映出一系列特殊的词语或表达方式,如"take to the streets, riot police, tear gas, concussion grenade, club, baton, truncheon, water cannon, rubber bullet, violent clash, casualties, dead, injured, detained, arrested, detainees, sympathy strike, sympathy demonstration, curfew, martial law"等,并通过逻辑关系把它们连接起来,形成一个完整的语义链。

当然,口译的过程是三种记忆方式共同作用的结果,切莫厚此薄彼,将三者割裂开来。此外,每个人的先天条件不同,可根据自身的特点加强练习。

四、习语翻译

汉语习语包括成语、俗语、谚语、歇后语等。有些诗词名句由于长期使用，已经家喻户晓，也变成了习语的一部分。习语简洁有力，寓意深刻，其特殊的结构和美妙的节奏使之成为语言中一个非常重要的组成部分。然而，汉英两种语言由于文化的差异，其习语的特点也有不同。如何处理好习语的翻译，是口译成败的关键。

（一）套用

汉英两种语言中，有很多习语无论从意象还是从意义的角度来说都是完全对等的。翻译时可直接套用。如：

沧海一粟 a drop in the bucket
趁热打铁 Strike while the iron is hot
百闻不如一见 Seeing is believing
有其父必有其子 Like father, like son
有志者事竟成 Where there is a will, there is a way
种瓜得瓜，种豆得豆 As you sow, so you reap
谋事在人，成事在天 Man proposes, Heaven disposes
吃一堑，长一智 A fall into the pit, a gain in your wit
嘴上无毛，办事不牢 A downy lip makes many a slip

（二）借用

汉英两种语言中有一类习语，尽管意象不同，但意义完全相同。由于口译"即时"的特点，译者没有充足的时间去"诠释"习语中的意象。因此，借用现成的表达方式是一个便捷、聪明的处理方法。如：

不入虎穴，焉得虎子 No pains, no gains.
乌鸦笑猪黑 The pot calls the kettle black.
江山易改，本性难移 Can a leopard change its spots?
近朱者赤，近墨者黑 He who keeps company with the wolf will learn to howl.
巧妇难为无米之炊 One cannot make bricks without straw.
只要功夫深，铁杵磨成针 Constant dropping wears away a stone.
只许州官放火，不许百姓点灯 One man may steal a horse while another may not look over a hedge.

（三）节译

汉语习语中，有一种为并列结构，即前半部分和后半部分意思完全一样。翻译时只要译出其中一部分即可。否则，拖泥带水，不符合英语习惯。如：

高谈阔论 empty talk
贪官污吏 corrupt officials

装疯卖傻 play the fool
甜言蜜语 honeyed words
摇唇鼓舌 wag one's tongue
咬牙切齿 grind one's teeth

（四）释译

有时套用或借用习语会产生文化冲突，此时，最安全的办法是释译，即舍弃形象，只译意思。比如，如果将"智者千虑，必有一失"译成"Even Homer sometimes nods"，很容易产生歧义，故套用中性的成语或者采取释译的方法就比较可取。故该成语可译成"No man is wise at all times"。其他例子如下。

指鹿为马 talk black into white

塞翁失马，焉知非福 a blessing in disguise

（五）诗词翻译

诗词在许多重要的领导人的发言中层出不穷，比比皆是。引用诗词一方面显示发言人知识渊博，同时说明其重视听众的文化程度。因此，平时积累常用诗词名句的翻译就显得非常重要。以下引语均出自外国领导人来华演讲。

（1）Long distance separates no bosom friends.

海内存知己，天涯若比邻。

（2）Isn't it a delight to have friends from afar?

有朋自远方来，不亦乐乎？

（3）So many deeds cry out to be done, and always urgently; the world rolls on, times presses. Ten thousand years are too long, seize the day, seize the hour!

多少事，从来急；天地转，光阴迫。一万年太久，只争朝夕。

（4）Promise, I pray, that someday when the task done, we go back to farming. We'll surely rent a plot of ground and as pairing neighbors let us live.

险夷不变应尝胆，道义争担敢息肩。待得归农功满日，他年预卜买邻钱。

类似例子不胜枚举。由于口译现场操作的特点，译者不可能去考虑韵脚节奏等，只能译出大意。因此，唯一补救的方法就是未雨绸缪，加强平时的积累。

（六）力避"假朋友"

所谓假朋友，是指字面意思相同而深层意思迥异的成语。比如，有人将"lock the stable door after the horse is stolen"译成"亡羊补牢"。从字面上看，非常对等。而实际上，二者的意思完全不同。"亡羊补牢"的寓意是"犹未为晚"。而英文成语却没有事后补救的意思。因此，"贼去关门"才是对等的翻译。再如，有人将"eat one's words"译成"食言"，而二者也仅仅是字面对等，其真实含义是"收回前言，承认错误"。"食言"的英语翻译应为"go back on one's words"。

五、词语精炼

英语中有句话，叫作"Brevity is the soul of wit"。汉语中有个成语，叫作"言简意赅"。二者表达的是同一个意思。这一观点在口译中尤为重要，这是因为口译受时间的限制，必须在最短的时间内把发言人的信息准确无误地传递出去。这就要求口译人员在平时多加练习，养成快速精炼的习惯。只有这样，才能在有限的时间内交出满意的答卷。

汉语因为节奏的原因，即"四字情结"，经常出现联合结构或者同义词堆砌的现象。此时，仅翻译一半即可（请参考习语翻译之"节译"）。如"跑冒滴漏"(leakage)、"铺天盖地"(overspread)、"南征北战"(fight on all fronts)、"东奔西走"(run around)、"男女老少"(men, women and children)、"夫妻老婆店"(mom-and-pop store)等。

有时为了加强语气，同义或近义的四字成语也常常叠用。对这类现象的处理方法依旧是"节译"。如"欣欣向荣、蒸蒸日上"(on the rise)、"班门弄斧、布鼓雷门"(teach fish to swim 或 teach a bird to sing 或 teach a spider to spin a web) 等。

还有一种现象，如"多快好省"与"少慢差费"等。这种四字结构和前面的两种情况有所不同，每个组成部分都有独立的含义。按字面翻译，前者应译为"more, faster, better, and more economical"；而后者则应译成"fewer, slower, poorer and more costly"。然而，在口译现场，"时间就是一切"，谁赢得了时间，谁就赢得了胜利，谁就能出色地完成任务。因此，可以考虑将它们分别译成"cost-effectively"和"inefficiently"。

汉语中很多表达方式本身就是一种"缩略语"，如"三从四德""三纲五常"等。它们本身有着丰富的含义。如果是笔译，我们完全可以采取脚注、尾注和内注的方式进行处理。

(1)"三从四德"可译为：

(a) the three types of obedience and four virtues

(b) three types of obedience (in ancient China a woman was required to obey her father before marriage, and her husband during married life and her sons in widowhood) and four virtues (fidelity, physical charm, propriety in speech and efficiency in needle work)

(2)"三纲五常"可以译为：

(a) the three cardinal guides and the five constant virtues as specified in the feudal ethical code

(b) the Three Cardinal Guides (ruler guides subject, father guides son and husband guides wife) and Five Constant Virtues (benevolence, righteousness, propriety, knowledge and sincerity)

试想一下，如果在口译（尤其是同声传译）现场采取上述翻译方法，结果会如何？因此，为了抢时间，抓要点，可以灵活处理成 wifely submission and virtue 和 principle of feudal moral conduct。

同样，很多政治词语的翻译也可借鉴以上方法。如"八荣八耻"可精炼为 socialist concept of honor and disgrace，而"五讲四美三热爱"可提炼为 socialist moral standards。

其他的例子如：

全心全意 wholeheartedly　　　　无法无天 unruly
三心二意 half-hearted　　　　　 五湖四海 everywhere
老弱病残 the infirm　　　　　　 五颜六色 colorful
形形色色 all sorts of　　　　　　林林总总 numerous

类似的例子，不胜枚举。关键是平时要善于积累，方可厚积薄发。

六、文化翻译

各个民族由于生存环境的不同，形成了迥异的文化及特殊的表达方式。因此，翻译时，必须考虑文化因素。否则，即使字面意思"相等"，也难以达意，甚至会南辕北辙。比如，intellectual 一词，字典释义为"知识分子"。其实，不是每一个受过教育的人都是 intellectual。在英语中，能够称得上的 intellectual 的人并不多，因为该词的真正含义是"高级知识分子"。因此，翻译时，切忌对号入座，望文生义。

（一）称呼上的差异

很多人将"这位是王厂长"译成"This is Director Wang"。乍一看完全对等，然而，不符合英语习惯。正确的翻译应为"This is Mr. Wang, our director"。这是因为英语中能够用头衔加姓直接称呼对方的表达方式并不多。常见的无非是 president、governor、mayor、judge、professor、Dr. 等。再如，"夫人"一词，在日常英语中可以译为 ma'am 或者 Mrs.，如 Mrs. White（怀特夫人）。然而，在正式场合，如国际会议上，"夫人"这个称呼并非 Mrs. 一词就可以完全解决的。也就是说，在很多情况下，Mrs. 就显得无能为力了。试比较下列说法。

（1）尼克松总统和夫人 Mr. President and Mrs. Nixon
（2）史密斯博士和夫人 Dr. and Mrs. Smith
（3）大使先生和夫人　Mr. Ambassador and Madame

在例（1）和例（2）中，都出现了姓氏，故译为 Mrs.。然而，在例（3）中没有出现姓氏，故译为 Madame。Madame 是尊称，如 Madame Curie（居里夫人）和 Madame Soong Ching Ling（宋庆龄夫人）等。

另外，"Dear Chinese friends""Dear Governor"中的 dear 不能想当然地译为"亲爱的"，而应根据汉语习惯译为"尊敬的"。

（二）问候语的差别

问候语是人际关系的"润滑油"。准确译好问候语常常是译文成功的关键。如，将"一路辛苦了"译成"You must be tired"或"You must have a tiring journey"纯属死译。这不但无法达意，反而可能引起反感。正确的译法应为"How's your trip？""Did you have a nice flight？"或者"Did you have a good journey？"。

再如，中国人见面一般会问三句话，"贵姓？""贵庚？"以及"在哪里高就？"。第一句话没有问题。第二句话在西方人眼里是禁忌，对女性来说尤其如此。因此，一般来说是不会问的。第三句话"在哪里高就？"初次见面时一般也很少有人问起。一定要问，也不能简单地将其译成"What's your job？"或者"What's your occupation？"这两种译法虽然字面对等，但不符合文化习惯，因为很多西方人没有固定的职业，直接发问的结果可能令对方尴尬。因此，比较得体的译法应为"What do you do for a living？"。

（三）套话的翻译

和问候语一样，套话的翻译必须符合习惯用法，否则，直译、死译、硬译必定会让人觉得生硬、死板，有时甚至会造成误解。比如：

（1）请大家多提宝贵意见。

如果将这句话译为"Your valuable suggestions, advice and criticism are always welcome / appreciated"或者"Please give us your valuable comments"，其结果只能是冷场。换言之，没有任何人会开口说话，因为谁也不知道自己的意见是否"宝贵"。因此，地道的翻译是将上述两个译文中的 valuable 一词去掉。

（2）今天的菜不好，请多多包涵。

中国人的特点是自谦。遇到类似表达方式绝对不可直译，否则给以虚伪的感觉。因此，如果是用餐开始时讲的，可译为"Bon appetite"或者"Please enjoy"；如果是用餐完毕时说的，则应译成"I hope you have enjoyed it"。

（3）讲得不好，请各位多多原谅。

这也是一句自谦的说法。如果直译，给听众以"不诚实"甚至是"蔑视"的感觉。因此，可以参照西方人的习惯，直接译成"Thank you for your attention（time）"。反过来，如果将英语发言人的结束语"Thank you for your attention（time）"直译成"谢谢大家的听讲"或者"谢谢大家的时间"，也显得生硬拗口，而且也不地道。所以，应根据汉语的习惯，简单译成"谢谢大家"即可。

（4）三句话。

"三句话"是很多身居要职的人的开场白，笔者在一次大型国际会议上就亲历了这一幕。当时，翻译简单地译成"Three sentences"。不料，发言人滔滔不绝，洋洋洒洒，岂止30句！场面好不尴尬。其实，碰到类似情况，根据具体情形完全可以灵活处理，如"I want to say/add a few words（about…）；I'd like to make a few remarks；Let me say a few words first；Now allow me to say a few words；

Let me just try to summarize here"等。

（5）姜还是老的辣。

国人常用这句话来恭维年长的人。一般情况下，可译成"Older and wiser" "The older the wiser"等。如果对方确系老人，当他说"I'm getting old. I am falling apart"时，你不妨说，"Old is good; The older, the wiser"，或者更客气一点说"The more senior, the wiser"。与国人喜欢论资排辈不同，西方人不愿意当"老大"，也就是说，不愿意说老，因为"老"总是和健康欠佳、机能减退等联系在一起。所以，当西方人碰到七八十岁的老人不得不问年龄时，他们会很诙谐地问道"How young are you?"。祝寿时会说"Oh, you are seventy-eight years young"。国人喜欢在姓前加"老"或者"小"以示亲切。国内的英语课本里，有的也相应地译成 Old Wang、Xiao Li。这些自以为清楚明白的中式英语到了英语里则变得不伦不类，非驴非马，不但无法达意，还容易引起误解。因此，我们不妨借助语言中的一种修辞现象委婉语来表达。比如"残疾人"，不要说"a disabled / crippled / handicapped person"，而要说"a physically-challenged person"或者干脆说"a challenged person"；"矮人"不是"a short person"，而是"a vertically-challenged person"；"胖人"不是"a fat person"，而是"a horizontally-challenged person"；"长相欠佳"不是"ugly"，而是"visually challenged"；"单身、孤单"不是"lonely"，而是"relationship-challenged"；"经济不宽裕"不是"poor"，而是"financially challenged"。再如，"老人"在英语里不说"old people"，而要说"senior adult"，"mature person"，"seasoned citizen"或者"golden-ager"，以示尊重。

（6）小小礼物，不成敬意，还望笑纳。

国人的最大特点是在外人面前"自谦"，而这在外事活动中构成了翻译的一道屏障。比如上面这句话，如果直译，则成了"This humble gift is not good enough to show my respect to you. I hope you will kindly take it"。结果如何呢？结果老外会满脸不悦，甚至觉得国人虚伪。明知不好，干吗送我呀？打发要饭的吗？这么好的东西还说不好，这不是虚伪吗？是不是要我感恩戴德呢？看，好事变成了坏事。其实，英语中有很多说法。最常见的是"Here's a little something for you. I hope you like it"。

（7）都在酒里了。

"都在酒里了"这句话是宴会期间最常见的一句话，在生意酒会上更是屡见不鲜。有人曾把它译为"We are all in the wine"。稍微有点常识的人都知道：一、这是不可能的，人怎么可能在酒里？二、国人喜欢泡药酒，里面蛇、乌龟什么都有，这样说，不是等于变相骂人吗？笔者在一家西餐馆用餐时，偶然看见一个烟灰缸上有三个英语单词 says it all。一看才知，这些烟灰缸是一家咖啡经营商送的，可见，是该咖啡的广告用语。咖啡可以用，酒为什么不可以呢？所以，当一个人举起酒杯为客人敬酒、口里说着"都在酒里了"时，不妨译成"It says it all"。此处的 it 当然指的是手里的酒。

（四）文化词的翻译

所谓文化词，指的是一种语言中特有的现象，包括风土人情、文化人物、历史事件等。由于口译自身的特点，译者不可能像笔译那样通过脚注或尾注的方式进行解释。因此，"内注"便成了译者的不二选择。不过，加内注时应注意做到言简意赅，切忌拖泥带水，喧宾夺主。内注得当会起到画龙点睛的作用。以下例句译文中的斜体部分均为内部注释。

（1）我喜欢太极，也喜欢武术。

I love Taiji, *or shadow boxing*, and wushu, *or martial arts* as well.

（2）四合院是北京的一大特色。

Siheyuan, *or courtyard buildings*, are part of Beijing.

（3）过端午节的时候，人们都吃粽子。

People eat zongzi, *a pyramid-shaped dumpling made of glutinous rice in bamboo or reed leaves*, during the Dragon-boat Festival.

（4）我去年参观过秦始皇陵。

Last year I visited the Mausoleum of Qinshihuang, *the first emperor of China*.

七、变词为句

英语中很多词或短语在翻译的时候可以根据汉语的习惯单独成句，或者成为独立成分。这种技巧常用于以下几种情形。

1. 现在分词、过去分词或分词短语用作定语或悬垂结构时，如"licensed and metered, crushing, as expected"等。

（1）Licensed and metered, all the taxis in the city provide good services.

该市所有的出租车都有运营执照，都安装了计价器，为客人提供优质服务。

（2）If non-performing loans reach the same level in Thailand, they will be a crushing 45% of GDP.

如果泰国的不良贷款达到相同水平，将占 GDP 总额的 45%，那对泰国经济来说将是致命一击。

（3）As expected, President Bush has signed a war spending bill. It was a bi-partisan effort that seems to have left both Democrats and Republicans unhappy.

果然不出所料，布什总统签署了军费支出议案。这是两党共同努力的结果，然而，民主党和共和党对此似乎都不满意。

（4）Qingdao, known as Switzerland in the East, is a beautiful coastal city.

青岛素有东方瑞士之称，是一座美丽的海滨城市。

2. 一些表达态度、看法的副词，如"arguably, undoubtedly, conspicuously,

obviously, incredibly, incidentally, sure enough, correctly"等。

(1) John is arguably the greatest captain in Chelsea's history already and I am certain he will do a fantastic job for England.

可以说，约翰是切尔西历史上最伟大的队长。我相信，在英格兰队他一定也会干得非常漂亮。

(2) Translating methods are undoubtedly the core problems we are confronted with in translation.

毫无疑问，翻译方法是翻译过程中所面临的核心问题。

(3) Women were conspicuously absent from the planning committee.

引人注意的是，规划委员会里没有一名女性委员。

(4) He obviously needed a wife.

显然，他需要成家了。

(5) He has an incredibly sharp memory.

他记忆力超群，令人难以置信。

(6) Dr. Watson, incidentally, was American-born, which shows that basic science is international.

顺便说一句，华生博士出生于美国，这表明基础科学具有国际性。

(7) Sure enough, the people of Israel are to be found everywhere today.

毫无疑问，当今以色列人在世界各地随处可见。

(8) Everywhere, you sense—correctly—that Cape Town is South Africa's most famous city.

无论在什么地方，你都会感到开普敦是南非最有名的城市。这种感觉是千真万确的。

3. 某些同位语表达成分，如"the capital city of Shandong Province, home to more than twenty ethnic groups"等。

(1) Jinan, the capital city of Shandong Province, is famous for its springs.

济南是山东省政府所在地，因泉水而闻名。

(2) Home to more than twenty ethnic groups, Yunnan Province lies in the south of China and abounds in fruits.

云南省是20多个少数民族的故乡，它位于中国南部，盛产水果。

4. 其他由 as, one of the many, one of the most 构成的特殊结构。

(1) The city government plans to divert 10 million yuan into preventing its youths from using drugs, as part of the city's drug control program.

该市计划拨款1000万元，防止青少年吸毒，这是该市禁毒计划的一部分。

(2) I rented a bike at one of the many shops which cost me a few dollars a day.

这里有很多自行车租赁店铺。我在其中一家租了一辆，每天的租金只有几美元。

八、数字翻译

数字翻译是口译中的一大重点，也是一大难点。说它是重点，是因为数字传递着重要的信息。说它是难点，是因为英汉两种语言在数字表达方式上不尽相同，或者说差异很大。这就要求译员平时要掌握规律，加强练习，从而达到融会贯通、游刃有余的地步。

（一）具体数字的翻译

1. 汉语的数字是以"十"的倍数来表示的，即个、十、百、千、万、十万、百万、千万、亿、十亿、百亿、千亿、万亿等，而英语的数字在"千"以内与汉语相同。

个 = one

十 = ten

百 = hundred

千 = thousand

在超过"千"以后，以"千"的倍数来表示：

一万 = ten thousand（十个千）

十万 = hundred thousand（百个千）

"百万"有对等的表达方式，million；"百万"以上的数字则用"百万"的倍数来表示：

千万 = ten million（十个百万）

亿 = hundred million（百个百万）

"十亿"有对等的表达方式，billion；"十亿"以上的数字则用"十亿"的倍数来表示。

百亿 = ten billion

千亿 = hundred billion

"万亿"（又叫"兆"）有对等的表达方式，trillion。

2. 百万以上的数字，最简便的方法是把"百万"以后的数字用"点"（即.）多少来表示。

960 万 = 9.6 million

8888 万 = 88.88 million

3. 如前所述，"亿"是一百个百万，因此，

567,890,000 = 567.89 million

4. 十亿以上的数字，最简便的方法是把"十亿"以后的数字用"点"（即.）多少来表示。

13 亿 = 1.3 billion

168 亿 = 16.8 billion

1234 亿 = 123.4 billion

5.万亿是 trillion，因此，万亿以后的数字，最简便的方法是把"万亿"以后的数字用"点"（即.）多少来表示。

56789 亿 = 5.6789 trillion

（二）非具体数字的翻译

所谓非具体数字的翻译，主要指的是一些笼统的数字。这些"数字"在日常生活中使用频率很高，需要熟练掌握。如：

几（若干）several，a few，some

十几 more than ten，over ten，no more than twenty，ten-odd（a ten-odd committee）

几十 dozens of

数以百计 hundreds of

数以千计 thousands of

数以万计 tens of thousands of

数十万 hundreds of thousands of

数百万 millions of

数千万 tens of millions of

亿万 hundreds of millions of

（三）具体数字的纪录方法

由于数字本身的重要性及其特殊性，有人总结出了"点三杠四"和"缺位补零"的记录方法。所谓"点三杠四"，或者"三位一点、四位一竖"，具体而言，就是"英文数字是三位一节，汉语数字是四位一节"。前者从右往左分别对应的是 thousand、million、billion 等，后者从右而左分别对应的是"万""亿"等。如：

one hundred twenty three million four hundred fifty six thousand seven hundred eighty nine

记录 1：123m 456 th 789

记录 2：1｜2345｜6789

记录 1 将声音准确记录下来。记录 2 根据汉语四位一节的特点自右而左标记出来，可以迅速准确读出数字为"一亿两千三百四十五万六千七百八十九"。再如：

八千七百六十五万四千三百二十一

记录 1：8765 万 4321

记录 2：87，654，321

记录 1 将声音准确记录下来。记录 2 根据英语三位一节的特点自右而左标记出来，可以迅速准确读出数字为 eighty-seven million six hundred fifty-four thousand three hundred twenty-one。

有时，数字中出现空位现象，如 fifty-four thousand and eighty-one，需要"缺位补零"。

记录1：54th 81

记录2：5｜4081

记录1中"零"没有体现出来。因此，为了准确，在翻译前需要像记录2一样把"零"补上。

汉译英也是一样的，如"八万六百四十五"可以标记如下。

记录1：8万645

记录2：80,645

同样，记录1中"零"没有体现出来。记录2补零以后，很容易就可以读出来。

九、词类转换

美国著名翻译理论家尤金·奈达说过，翻译是翻译意思。换言之，翻译不是简单的词语对等，也不是对原文结构的临摹。因此，在实际翻译过程中，应根据译入语的需要，进行词类转换。如：

（1）他烧得一手好菜。

He's a great cook.

（2）她晕船。

She's a bad sailor.

（3）This is a booklet on the details about our department.

这里有一本小册子，详细介绍了我系的情况。

（4）I'm sorry he's out at the moment.

很抱歉，他此刻不在。

从以上例句中不难看出，译文均从某种意义上进行了词类转换。也只有这样，才能使译文地道通顺。这里着重介绍英译汉时经常出现的词类转换情况。

（一）介词转换成动词

（1）I'm all for it.

我举双手赞成。

（2）All peace-loving people are strongly against arms race.

一切爱好和平的人们都强烈反对军备竞赛。

（二）名词转化成动词

（1）The sight of the snake made his hair stand on end.

一看到蛇，他便毛发倒竖，头皮发麻。

（2）The little girl pales at the mere mention of dogs.

一提到狗，小女孩吓得脸都白了。

(3) As a result, importance is attached to the inculcation and accumulation of knowledge, respect to authority, cultivation of students' rigor and preciseness in learning.

因而，（中国教育）注重传授和积累知识，尊重权威，培养学生的严谨学风。

(4) Reflections of the new system are different.

这个新的体制，人们反响不一。

（三）副词转化成动词

(1) He wasn't in when you called.

你来电话的时候，他出去了。

(2) Five days later, the patient was up and about again.

5天后，病人又开始下地走动了。

（四）形容词转化成动词

(1) She was asleep the whole day.

她睡了整整1天。

(2) Mary was sure that she had given the book to Tom.

玛丽肯定自己把书给了汤姆。

（五）名词转换成形容词

(1) Insecurity and turbulence appear all-pervasive.

举国上下，危机四伏，动荡不安。

(2) The plan was a complete success.

计划非常成功。

（六）形容词转变为副词

(1) The plane landed safe.

飞机安全着陆。

(2) That's sheer nonsense.

那纯粹是一派胡言。

（七）副词转换成形容词

(1) Traditionally, the two countries had good relations.

两国一直保持着传统友谊。

(2) They had fully prepared for the exam.

他们为考试做好了充分准备。

（八）副词转换成名词

(1) Physically weak as he was, he worked very hard.

他尽管身体虚弱，但工作非常卖力。

(2) He is a mentally sound man, though.

尽管如此，他依然是一个思想健康的人。

（九）形容词转变成名词

（1）He was a very eloquent speaker.
他口才很好。

（2）The rich should not look down upon the poor.
富人不该看不起穷人。

其实，在翻译实践中还有很多种类型的词类转换。关键是译者要着眼于译入语的行文习惯，灵活处理。汉译英时也不例外，应根据英语的行文习惯，酌情处理。

十、词语省略

有人认为，汉语是文学的语言，英语是科学的语言，这种说法不无道理。这是因为汉语靠意思连贯（意合），英语靠句法成句（形合）。也就是说，除个别情况外，英语句子的句法形式与功能必须是完整的。例如，含有及物动词的句子，必须有主语、谓语和宾语，缺一不可。

无论是汉语也好，英语也罢，在翻译时都必须根据译入语的习惯进行增减。所谓省略，是删去一些可有可无的词，绝不是任意删减，更不是删去原文的信息内容。

从汉译英的角度来看，省略重点有三大类。

（一）省略表示范畴的词语

汉语中的一些范畴词，如"问题、现象、状态、面貌、事业、制度、局面、情况、工作、任务"等，本身没有实质意义，翻译时可以省去不译。如：

（1）新中国成立以来，尤其是改革开放后，我国的经济发展取得了举世瞩目的成就，但贫困问题依旧是当前不可回避的一个现实问题。

Since the founding of the People's Republic of China，and especially since reform and opening-up，great achievements have been made in China's economic development. However，poverty is inevitably a serious problem.

（2）市政府正在采取积极措施解决失业问题。

The municipal government is taking active measures to deal with unemployment.

（3）本文介绍了中国的人口状况。

The essay touches upon the population in China.

（4）出现紧急情况，请走楼梯。

In case of an emergency，please use the stairs.

（5）《联合国气候变化框架公约》及其《京都议定书》凝聚了各方的广泛共识，是国际合作应对气候变化的法律基础和行动指南。

The United Nations Framework Convention on Climate Change and the Kyoto Protocol reflect the broad consensus among all parties and serve as the legal basis and guide for international cooperation on climate change.

(6) 中国人民的面貌、社会主义中国的面貌发生了历史性变化。
Historic changes have taken place in the Chinese people and socialist China.

(二) 省略原文中重复出现的词语

汉语不怕重复，然而，这却是英语行文的大忌。因此，翻译时，原文中重复出现的词语可使用代词替代，或干脆省略不译。如：

(1) 长征是历史纪录上的第一次，长征是宣言书，长征是宣传队，长征是播种机。
The Long March is the first of its kind in the annals of history. It is a manifesto, a propaganda force and a seeding-machine.

(2) 全国社会稳定，政治稳定，处处呈现出生机勃勃的景象。
Social and political stability throughout the country makes for a vibrant outlook.

(三) 省略修饰语

汉语中有很多修饰语，主要为副词和形容词，其作用是加强语气，如"隆重庆祝""正式开幕""胜利闭幕""欢聚一堂"等，翻译成英语时可直接省略。如：

(1) 我宣布第20届洛阳牡丹花会正式开幕。
I declare the opening of the twentieth Luoyang Peony Festival.

(2) 今天，我们在这里欢聚一堂，热烈欢迎史密斯先生。
We are here today to give Mr. Smith a warm welcome.

(3) 今天，我们在这里集会，隆重庆祝中华人民共和国成立60周年。
We are gathered together here today to celebrate the 60th anniversary of the founding of the People's Republic of China.

(4) 遏制气候变暖，拯救地球家园，是全人类共同的使命。
It is the common mission of the entire mankind to curb global warming and save our planet.

从英译汉的角度来看，省略的种类较多，如冠词、代词、人称代词、非人称代词、物主代词、并列连词、从属连词、介词、重复词、修饰语等。

(四) 省略从属连词、关系代词/副词

汉语中的逻辑关系往往隐含在句子中，由语序加以体现。因此，有时可以省略英语中一些表示原因、条件或时间的从属连词，以及关系从句中的关系代词/副词。如：

(1) I can't go now because I'm very busy.
我很忙，这会儿去不了。

(2) If I had known it, I wouldn't have done that.
早知如此，绝对不会那么做。

(3) When I turned round, I saw her running toward me.
我转过身来，看见她正朝我跑来。

（4）She wept as she spoke.
她边说边哭。

（5）When a certain species is affected by our chemicals, entire food chains are disrupted.
某一物种受到化学物质的影响，会导致整个食物链的失衡。

（6）This sets off a chain reaction where the permanent changes in weather bring calamities such as the rise to diseases that once could not thrive in cold climates, the destruction of specific ecosystems, desertification and unpredictable weather.
这引起了连锁反应，气候的恒久变化引发灾难。例如，以前在寒冷地带鲜见的某些疾病的发病率上升，对特殊物种生态系统的破坏，土壤荒漠化以及变幻无常的气候。

（五）以信息对等为基础，译语的略译处理

这主要是由译语的行文习惯决定的，省略后既保留了原语的信息，又使译语简洁、自然、地道。如：

（1）And the experts agree it will take a couple of weeks for everyone to get used to his or her own bed, and that it will get worse before it gets better, but success can be achieved.
专家一致认为，大家需要几周的时间才能适应自己的床，而且情况会暂时变得更糟，不过终究会成功的。

（2）Our emissions of sulfur and nitrogen produce a phenomenon called acid rain, which is harmful to plants and animals that live in the water.
硫黄和氮气的排放，造成了酸雨现象，危及水生动植物。

（3）应对气候变化必须在可持续发展的框架下统筹安排，决不能以延续发展中国家的贫穷和落后为代价。
Action on climate change must be taken within the framework of sustainable development and should by no means compromise the efforts of developing countries to get rid of poverty and backwardness.

为达到加强语气或表达优美的目的，汉语经常使用结构对称而信息重叠的表达，英译时可略译。如：

（1）近朱者赤，近墨者黑。
Touch pitch and you will be defiled.
（2）聚精会神搞建设，一心一意谋发展
concentrate on development
（3）吸纳百家优长，兼集八方精义
call for drawing upon the strength of others

十一、词语增补

前面说过，汉语是意合的语言，英语是形合的语言。因此，汉译英时，增补便成了必不可少的手段。

（一）增补主语

汉语中的无主句在翻译时必须补出"所谓的"主语。在下面的例子中，斜体部分为增补部分，否则，不符合英语的行文习惯。如：

（1）下雨了。

It is raining.

（2）8点了。起床吧，懒鬼。

It's eight o'clock. Get up, you lazybones.

（二）增补连接词

汉语，尤其是口语中，在很多场合都省略连词。译成英语时，需要根据情况增补。如：

（1）你去我就去。否则，我宁愿待在家里。

I'll go *if* you are going. *If not*, I'd rather stay at home.

（2）昨晚下雨了，今早地都湿了。

It rained last night, *for* the ground is wet this morning.

（三）根据语境、事实、逻辑关系等因素增补适当的词语

（1）她起床后，穿好衣服，直接奔往灾区。

She got up, put on *her* clothes, and made straight for the disaster area.

（2）大连是一个经济发达的沿海开放城市。

Dalian is a coastal city with a *fairly* developed economy.

（3）我们的使命就是要全面建设小康社会。

Our mission is to build a *moderately* well-off society in an all-round way.

（4）青岛在轻纺方面有着传统优势。

Qingdao enjoys traditional strengths in *textile and other light industries*.

（5）我们的周边国家和地区纷纷以较低的价格吸引客户。

Some manufacturers from our neighboring countries and regions have attracted the customers with lower prices.

（6）联合国项目

UN-*sponsored* programs

（7）美元资产

US dollar-*denominated* assets

英语通常非常简洁，言简意赅。然而，如果逐字逐句翻译过来总觉得意犹未尽，行文欠妥。此时，增补就变得十分必要。

1. 在下面的例子中，如果没有括号里的文字，便不符合汉语习惯。如：

（1）The global economy is a fact.
经济全球化是个（不争的）事实。

（2）Throughout my term as Secretary-General, I have sought to place human beings at the center of everything we do — from conflict prevention to development to human rights.
在我担任秘书长期间，我总是坚持以人为本的方针，从预防冲突到（谋求）发展，（再）到（维护）人权，（无不如此）。

（3）Thank you for your invitation and hospitality.
感谢您的（盛情）邀请和（热情）款待。

（4）Education in Britain is compulsory. All children must go to school from the age of five to sixteen. That's the law.
英国实行义务教育。5至16岁的孩子都必须上学。这是法律（规定的）。

（5）Thanks you for your words of welcome.
感谢您（热情洋溢）的欢迎词。

（6）Welcome to Qingdao—The Island City.
欢迎到青岛来。（欢迎到）"岛城"（来）。

2. 很多抽象名词在翻译时需要增补适当的词语。如：

（1）They were busy making final preparations for the exam.
他们正在为考试做着最后的准备（工作）。

（2）UNAIDS Executive Director Peter Piot said that in the world who are still widespread poverty, many of the hungry, grain prices soaring and food shortage is a serious threat to the fight against AIDS.
联合国艾滋病规划署执行主任彼得·皮奥特说，在世界上那些贫困（现象）仍很普遍、饥民众多的地区，粮价飞涨和食品供应不足正严重威胁着抗击艾滋病行动。

（3）The crew members were able to deal with all kinds of emergencies.
机组成员可以应付任何紧急（情况）。

（4）Despite the pressure from the interest groups, the Obama Administration publicly urged an easing of tensions with Iran.
顶着利益集团的巨大压力，奥巴马政府公开主张缓和同伊朗的紧张（关系）。

十二、语境定义

英文中有一句名言，叫作"词本无意，意由境生"（No context, no text），足见上下文在阅读乃至翻译中的重要作用。比如"Time flies"，一看到这句话，大多数人会不约而同地将其译成"时间飞逝"。其实，离开了上下文，很难说这是一个正确的翻译，因为这句话至少还有另外一个意思，那就是"测一下苍蝇的飞行速度。"以下例句都离不开上下文，必须在特定的语境中获取其特殊的含义。

（1）The dog had an accident on the rug.

"accident"最常见的意思是"事故"。如果将其译成"狗在地毯上出事故了"，比较令人费解。这里，"on the rug"排除了"accident"作为"事故"解的意思。也正是因为"on the rug"这个特殊的语境，该句的正确译文应为"狗拉在地毯上了"。

（2）Surprise Attack on Pearl Harbor

著名的珍珠港事件改变了太平洋战争的态势，为人们留下了无尽的思考。然而，"Surprise Attack on Pearl Harbor"究竟应如何翻译？这主要取决于作者的身份及立场。如果作者是美国人，且是珍珠港事件的幸存者，那么，应毫不犹豫地译成"偷袭珍珠港"。但是，也有文献不这么翻译，而是字面上略作改动，译作"奇袭珍珠港"。一字之差，情感含义天壤之别。

（3）The party was over. Everybody was longing for a horizontal position.

有人将此句译成"晚会结束了，每个人都渴望一种水平位置"。译文给人以不知所云的感觉。何为"水平位置"？其实，结合"晚会结束了"这句话不难看出，"a horizontal position"是"躺下来休息"的意思，因为大家都玩累了。因此，正确的译文应为，"晚会结束了，大家都想躺下来休息休息"。

（4）The small boat disappeared into the horizon.

有人将这句话译成"小船消失在地平线上"。"horizon"可以表示"地平线"，也可以表示"海平面"。"地平线"是天地交接的地方。所以，船无论如何也不可能消失在"地平线"上。因此，该句应译成"小船消失在水天相接的地方"。

（5）The Memorandum of Understanding was signed in May by the Corporation of London and the Shanghai Municipality.

本句的焦点在于"corporation"一词。该词最常见的意思是"公司"。如果认为谅解备忘录是由伦敦公司和上海市政府签署的，有悖于常识。根据上下文以及外交对等的原则，"the Corporation of London"应为"伦敦市政府"。

（6）Britain is a whole-hearted supporter of free trade since the Gatt's establishment. We remain an unashamed champion of free trade today.

"champion"有"冠军、勇士、战士、捍卫者、保护者、支持者"等意思。本例的前一句是"自关贸总协定成立以来，英国一直是自由贸易的忠实的支持者"。根据该句构成的语境，"champion"的意思不言自明，应该是"倡导者、捍卫者"。所以，第二句应译为"如今，我们依然是自由贸易公开的捍卫者"。

（7）A：I got a ticket yesterday.

B：Welcome to the club.

译文：A：我昨天收到一张罚单。

B：欢迎来到俱乐部。

这种译文读后让人如堕五里雾中。收到罚单与俱乐部之间有什么关系？根据语境,我们知道,第二句话的意思应是"同病相怜""同是天涯沦落人"之意,因此,应该译为"我也一样啊!"或者"我们是难兄难弟啊!"。

(8) 下列例子都与 "killer" 有关。由于搭配不同,其含义也不同。

He's got a killer smile.

The green skirt is a real killer.

The English exam was a real killer.

killer 原意为"杀手",并由此衍生出很多意思。根据不同的搭配,三句话的意思分别是:

他的微笑很迷人。

那件绿裙子真好看。

英语考试难得不得了。

(9) 下列例句的翻译都与金融危机的语境相关。

Comparing economic statistics is inevitably a "glass is half empty" versus "glass is half full" kind of game. Both Pollyannas and Cassandras can marshal endless statistics to support their version of events.

对比经济数据不可避免地成了"杯子半空"对"杯子半满"式的游戏,乐观和悲观的经济预言家们都可无休止地列举数据,用以支持各自的观点。

Uncertainty means that it is reasonable to pull your horns in a bit—and diversify away from stocks, emphasizing a diverse group of assets that are less correlated to the stock market.

经济的不确定性意味着应适当限制投资行为,应规避股票,使资产投资多样化,并尽量不涉及股市。

The top hedge managers I know are more focused on playing defense until the dust settles.

我认识的高层对冲基金经理更注重规避风险,谨慎行事,静待经济恢复正常。

十三、长句处理

总的来说,汉语中短句居多,而英语则以长句见长。英译汉时,如果句子过长,一方面不符合汉语习惯,另一方面会给译者增加负担,同时也给听众增加压力。因此,必须对其进行"切割"处理,即断句。断句的前提是"意群",而切割后如何衔接是口译成败的关键。

造成英译汉句子冗长的主要原因在于译者不知断句,定语过长。初学者往往死译原文结构,且前后颠倒,结果译文拖沓,逻辑不清,影响理解。因此,如何处理好原文较长的定语/同位语或定语/同位语从句,如何做到化整为零,是对口译人员顺译能力的一大考验。如:

(1) The notion that the source of East Asia's rapid economic growth has per-

manently dried up is simply wrong.（同位语从句）

译文一：那种认为东亚经济快速增长的源头已经彻底枯竭的想法是完全错误的。

译文二：有人认为，东亚经济快速增长的源头已经彻底枯竭，这种想法是完全错误的。

比较两种译文，不难看出，译文一尽管忠实于原文的意思，但生吞活剥原文的结构，其结果是不听完最后一个字很难知道全句的意思，这无形中增加了听众的压力。相反，译文二采用顺译的方法，并通过增词和词类转换的手段，前后连接，干脆利落，层次分明，地道通顺。类似的例句如下。

(2) The old idea that anyone with a little money can start a business and operate it successfully is no longer valid.（同位语从句）

译文一：那种认为任何人只要有一点钱就可以创业并且经营得很好的旧观念已经过时了。

译文二：过去有人认为，任何人只要有一点资金就可以成功创业，这种观念已经过时了。

译文三：过去有人认为，任何人都可以白手起家，这种观念已经过时了。

译文一生硬拖沓；译文二通顺地道；译文三简洁流畅。

(3) At our party conference last year I said the task to change the national attitude of mind was the most challenging to face for any British Administration since the war.（动词不定式短语作定语）

译文一：在我们去年的党大会上我说过，改变国民思想态度的任务对战后任何一届英国政府来说都是最富挑战性的。

译文二：在去年的党大会上，我曾经说过，我们所面临的任务就是要改变国民的态度。这项任务十分艰巨，是战后历届英国政府都未曾遇到的。

译文一佶屈聱牙，生搬硬套。译文二采用断句增补的方法，自然流畅，一气呵成。

(4) More than 2,000 entries are submitted each year in the Pulitzer Prize competition, and only 21 awards are normally made. The awards are the culmination of a year-long process that begins early in the year with the appointment of 102 distinguished judges who serve on 20 separate juries and are asked to make 3 nominations in each of the 21 categories.（第二句中含有两个定语从句）

译文一：每年有超过2000件入选作品参加普利策奖的竞争，但通常只颁发21个奖项。这些奖项是长达1年过程的终结。它始于每年年初，受委派的102名杰出的评审员分成20个评审团，在21个项目中各提名3件作品。

译文二：每年都有2000多件作品角逐普利策奖，但通常只设21个奖项。评奖过程为期一年，从年初开始。共有102位著名的评委，分成20个小组，要求他们在21大类中各推举3件作品。

译文一是典型的死译，是穿着汉语外衣的英语。译文二既忠于原文的意思，又通顺流畅。两相比较，孰优孰劣，不言自明。

汉语长句多见于政论和科技文章，总的原则依然是顺译，同时，根据实际情况，灵活变通。如：

(1) 香港回归后，将继续保持自由港的地位，继续发挥国际金融、贸易、航运中心的作用，继续同各国各地区及有关国际组织发展经济文化关系。

After the return, Hong Kong will retain its status of a free port, continue to function as an international financial, trade and shipping center, and maintain and develop its economic and cultural ties with other countries, regions and relevant international organizations.

(2) 一些希腊的哲学家们认为，一切物质都是由四种元素构成的，即土、火、空气和水。于是，很多人就认为，如果把这些元素重新组合的话，一种物质就可能变成另一种物质。

Some Greek philosophers held that all matter was made up of the same four "elements"—earth, fire, air and water; and many people therefore thought that if these elements could be rearranged, one substance could be changed into another.

十四、语态转换

英语中被动句的使用比较广泛，而汉语中主动句的使用则比较普遍。因此，在翻译过程中，应根据两种语言在语态方面的差异，进行适当调整，以期符合两种语言的行文特点，使译文更加地道自然。

汉语被动句往往含有"负面"的意思，如不愉快、不如意等。因此，使用起来应十分小心。相反，英语被动语态则无此禁忌，或褒或贬或中性，使用范围不受限制。因此，英译汉时，切忌对号入座，盲目照抄照搬原文结构。

1. 英语被动句在绝大多数情况下可以译成汉语主动句。

比较下列例句两种不同的译法，不难看出，前者生硬死板，后者流畅自然。

(1) I went to the office and was told that the meeting was cancelled.

a. 我到了办公室，被告知会议取消了。

b. 我到了办公室，得知（获悉）会议取消了。

(2) He was promoted to be the CEO of the Haier Group.

a. 他被提拔为海尔集团首席执行官。

b. 他荣升海尔集团首席执行官。

(3) This book has been translated into twenty languages.

a. 该书已被译成二十种语言。

b. 该书已经译成二十种语言。

（4）And this will be dealt with in the next chapter.

a. 这一点将在下一章被讨论。

b. 这一点将在下一章讨论。

（5）Professor Smith is known to us for his great achievements in the study of nanotechnology.

a. 史密斯教授被我们大家所熟知，他在纳米技术研究方面成绩斐然。

b. 史密斯教授我们大家都很熟悉，他在纳米技术研究方面成绩斐然。

（6）According to the regulations, foreign tourists are not allowed to take objects out of China for other people.

a. 根据规定，外国游客不被允许为他人将物品带出中国。

b. 根据规定，外国游客不得为他人将物品带出中国。

2. 下列英语特殊结构可以译成汉语中的无主句。

It is said that ... 据说……

It is reported ... 据报道……

It is hoped that ... 希望……

It is estimated that... 估计……

It must be admitted that ... 必须承认……

It is well known that... 众所周知……

It is thought that... 人们认为……

It is suggested that ... 建议……

It must be remembered that ... 必须记住……

3. 特定情况下一定要译成被动语言，尽量减少"被"字的使用，代之以地道的汉语表达方式。常常用来替换"被"字的词或词组有"挨""遭""遭到""使""为……所""受到"等。

（1）They were frequently beaten and were forced to live in prison-like conditions.

他们经常挨打，被迫在监牢般的环境中生活。

（2）In that case, even if your credit card is stolen, your money is still there.

这样，即使信用卡失窃，你的钱依然完好无损。

（3）The enemy submarine was crippled.

敌人的潜艇受到重创。

（4）The United States had been known as a melting pot.

美国素有"大熔炉"之称。

（5）Many books, like Follow Me, Family Album, USA, are well received.

很多书，如《跟我学》《走遍美国》，都很受欢迎。
（6）He was not swayed by her good looks.
他不为其美貌所动。
4. 汉语中的无主句可以译成英语被动语态。
（1）办公楼内禁止吸烟。
Smoking is not allowed in the office building.
（2）此处要建造一座80层的金融中心。
An eighty-story financial center will be built here.
（3）苏里南说什么语言？
What language is spoken in Surinam？
（4）冬天必须保证充足的煤炭供应。
A sufficient supply of coal should be guaranteed in winter.
（5）在解决东海问题时，不仅要考虑中日两国的眼前利益，也要考虑到该地区的长期利益。
Consideration should be given to both the immediate interests of China and Japan，but also the long-term interests of the whole region in dealing with the East China Sea issue.
（6）最后，必须指出，保护环境人人有责。
Finally，it must be pointed out that it is everybody's responsibility to protect the environment.
5. 汉语中以泛指性主语为开头的句子可以译成英语被动语态。
（1）人们常说，熟能生巧。
It is often said that practice makes perfect.
（2）有人认为，联合国这个名字是由美国总统富兰克林·D·罗斯福提出来的。
The name "United Nations" is thought to have been put forward by US President Franklin D. Roosevelt.
（3）人们普遍认为，孩子的成长需要营养，同样也离不开鼓励。
It is generally accepted that a child is fed by milk and praise as well.
（4）众所周知，花生一开始是喂猪的。
It is well known that peanuts were first used as pig feed.

十五、正反变通

正反变通是非常重要的翻译方法，无论是汉译英，还是英译汉，都是如此。理由很简单。同样一句话，可以正说，也可以反说。比如，Staff Only 在不同场合有不同的翻译。如果是超市电梯门或者厕所门上的标识语，可以直译成"员工专用"。如果是商场、图书馆等其他场合的标识语，则可以反译为"顾客止步"，这样更符合汉语的习惯。同样,"小心地滑"(商场)、"下雨路滑"(高速公路)、"油漆未干"等警示语,也可以用反译的方法,使之更符合英语警示语的行文方式。因此,可分别译成"Wet floor""Wet road"和"Wet Paint"。有时,根据不同的上下文或译入语的行文习惯,只能进行正反变通,否则,译文便佶屈聱牙,难以达意。比如,"criminal police"不是"犯罪警察"而是"刑警"。同样,"riot police"不是"暴力警察",而是"防暴警察"。上述两个例子充分说明,反译法有时是必须的,否则,必然造成错译误译。为了更好地说明问题,请看以下例句。

(一)英译汉

(1) I couldn't agree more.

我举双手赞成。

(2) This sort of situation highlights a critical weakness in the ANC leadership:accountability.

这突出地反映了非国大领导人一个极其严重的弱点,即玩忽职守。

(3) With a century of twists and turns behind us, it is not surprising that there is uncertainty in both the United States and China about the future of our responsibility.

过去的一百年并非一帆风顺,难怪美中两国对未来关系的走向都心存疑虑。

(4) This attitude provides a firm foundation that will support the relationship despite tremors and storms.

这种态度为两国关系奠定了坚实的基础,使之能够经受住狂风骤雨的考验。

(5) Your exhibits are very attractive, though the workmanship is not so desirable.

贵方的展品颇有吸引力,不过,工艺还有待提高。

(6) I promise I will become a Chinese expert in no time.

我保证很快就会成为中国通。

(7) They made the fire within no small difficulty.

他们费了好大的劲儿才把火生了起来。

(二)汉译英

(1) 你已经不小了,知道这种场合该怎么做了。

You are old enough to know what to do on such an occasion.

(2) 问题依然存在。

The problem remained unsolved.

(3) 回家的路上别忘了替我把信寄出去。

Remember to post the letter for me on your way home.

(4) 加倍小心。

You can never be too careful.

（5）中国如此，世界也不例外。

What is true of China is also true of the world.

（6）美国素有"大熔炉"之称，因为很多人的祖先是移民。他们来自世界各地，在这片新大陆上定居。

The United States is known as a melting pot because many of its people are descendents of settlers who came from all over the world to make their homes in the new land.

（7）听说在美国能赚大钱，而且有宗教自由和政治自由，世界各地的人们蜂拥而至，来到美国。

Attracted by reports of great economic opportunities and religious and political freedom, immigrants from all over the world flocked to the United States.

十六、随机应变

掌握了所有"对策"，并不代表可以顺利完成任务，关键在于临场发挥，随机应变。这种能力需要在大量的实践活动中"养成"，即平时加强训练，在大量练习中将口译技能融会贯通，更要注意多积累各方面的知识，加强复述能力，处乱不惊，始终保持平衡心态。知识积累和心态平衡对于同声传译来说，尤为如此。以下例证主要从这两方面强调了随机应变能力的培养。

（1）下面是笔者的一次亲身经历。

某政府官员在推销自己城市的旅游业时，是这样说的：

大力发展旅游业……（接下来是毫无原因的停顿）

因为是同声传译，笔者马上译为 To promote tourism in（城市名）。此时，该官员如梦方醒，突然说道：

……的目的是……

如果是交替传译，不会成为任何问题，可以等句子完整后再译，比如：

The aim / goal /purpose/ target of promoting tourism in ... is ...

然而，同传不允许你从头来过。那怎么办呢？此时，平时的积累就起着关键的作用。笔者当时灵机一动，很自然地用了 is aimed to/at 这个短语，故整个句子变成了

To promote tourism in ... is aimed at...

当然，除了这一表达方式之外，还可应用 is targeted to 等。其他场合表示"目的"，还可以用 is intended for、is designed for、seeks to 等。这再次说明"台上一分钟、台下十年功"的说法包含着多少辛苦、多少磨炼。

（2）再举一个例子：中央政府大力支持这个计划。

句子中"大力支持"，既可以用动词（strongly）support 来翻译，也可以用动词短语来翻译，如 give（full / strong）support to，还可以用介词短语 in support of 或形容词短语 supportive of 译之。也就是说，译者可以根据具体情况，灵活选择。

换言之，对于一个出色的译员来说，任何一句话都应有两种或多种表达方式。唯有这样，才能临阵不乱，从容自若。

（3）下面列举几个实例，供初学者参考。

A. 天无绝人之路。

There is always a way out.

Heaven never seals off all exits.

Every cloud has a silver lining.

Heaven will always leave a door open.

B. 近水楼台先得月。

It is always easy to fetch water when the river is near.

First come，first served.

A waterfront pavilion gets the moonlight first.

A baker's wife may bite of a bun，a brewer's wife may bite of a tun.

C. 优点和缺点（利弊）

strong points and weak points

strengths and weaknesses / shortcomings / drawbacks

advantages and disadvantages

merits and demerits

pros and cons

D. 我请客。

It's my treat.

It's on me.

Let me pay.

I'm paying.

I'm treating.

I'm treating you.

I got it.

I'll get it.

Let me treat.

Let me pay the bill.

Let me foot the bill.

I'll pick up the tab.

Let me treat you.

I want to treat.

I want to treat you.

Let me buy you lunch.

Don't say a word. Next time you can pay.